NO-NONSENSE DELEGATION

NO-NONSENSE
DELEGATION

DALE D. McCONKEY

A DIVISION OF AMERICAN MANAGEMENT ASSOCIATIONS

Library of Congress Cataloging in Publication Data

McConkey, Dale D
 No-nonsense delegation.

 1. Delegation of authority. I. Title.
 HD38.M28   658.4   73-93670
 ISBN 0-8144-5361-9

International standard book number: 0-8144-5361-9
Library of Congress catalog card number: 73-93670

Twelfth printing

PREFACE

PROBABLY NO PART of the management process is more misunderstood than delegation. Every manager, to one degree or another, has his own definition. Some equate delegation with abdication. For others, it means handing out detailed job assignments. Still others believe it involves parceling out work while retaining authority. The right to make decisions often is not considered necessary. Still others cling to the time-honored theory that accountability cannot be delegated.

Many managers really don't appreciate why they should delegate. It's merely something the books say should be done. They believe some importance must be attached to delegation because so much has been written and spoken about it. But they lack the *why* and *how*.

Much of this confusion undoubtedly results from the popular, but inadequate, definition of delegation. Usually, delegation is defined as "getting things done through other people." The primary weaknesses of this definition are that it fails to consider the quality and quantity of the "things" and the how and when these "things" will be achieved.

This book begins by redefining the manager's job. He must insure the accomplishment of economically significant results. This definition overcomes the weaknesses of the old definition. The quality and quantity of accomplishment and how and when it takes place are now included. Achieving the results through effective delegation becomes our goal.

No-Nonsense Delegation deals with the real "guts" of delegation. I hope it will help managers at all levels to achieve better results through effective delegation. I hope, too, that in the process managers and their subordinates will have been provided with the opportunity and vehicle for contributing in a more significant, meaningful, and self-rewarding manner. Such is my intent.

I am indebted to my secretary, Mary A. Vance, for the conscientious manner in which she performed the typing and administrative duties connected with this book. Thanks, Mary.

Dale D. McConkey

CONTENTS

1	What Is a Manager?	1
2	Why Delegate?	16
3	Symptoms of Poor Delegation	32
4	Causes of Poor Delegation	46
5	Building the Foundation for Delegation	64
6	The Truths of Delegation	80
7	The Role of the Delegator	90
8	The Role of the Delegatee	100
9	What Delegation Requires of the Job Description	109
10	Delegation by Levels	124
11	Authority That Gets Results	137
12	Establishing Dynamic Controls	155
13	Delegation and Decision Making	168
14	Developing Managers Through Delegation	180
15	Evaluation of Delegation	194
16	The Demand for Accountability and Participation	206
	Appendix	215
	Index	221

[1]

WHAT IS A MANAGER?

THE MANAGER'S JOB—or portions of it—is delegated. Before the delegation takes place, we must determine what a manager is. A satisfactory answer must include what a manager is specifically accountable for; how he justifies his continued existence in the organization; and how he can better demonstrate the worth and need for his job. Only then can he delegate parts of his responsibility.

Too often, unsuccessful efforts have been made to delegate first and to decide the role of the manager later. Equally unsuccessful attempts have been made to determine the job as the delegation unfolded.

One major obstacle to effective delegation is the commonly accepted definition of management: "Management is getting things done through other people." The definition is inadequate, misleading, and overly general. It fails to describe the real purpose of management. It suggests that a sales manager who directs his salesmen so that sales increase 100 percent but who secures the sales increase without due regard to the gross margin on the sales is managing. Or that an antiunion plant manager whose sentiments are carried out by his managers to the extent that a costly strike results is managing. The definition is also met by the research director and his professionals who for years have squandered huge sums on unprofitable research projects.

Similarly—and of prime importance to any consideration of delegation—the definition's requirements are met by the autocratic boss who calls all his managers together each morning and proceeds to hand each manager his assignment for the day on a "you do this, you do that, do it this way" basis. He's managing—but not really! His managers are actually no more than order-receivers and carry-outers. Even though he may get things done through other people, essentially he's asking other people to carry out his decisions, not to manage. Managing requires decision making and a healthy amount of self-initiated action.

Finally, let's apply the definition to the top manager—the president. He calls in his research manager and says to him, "You're in charge of research, go out and do some researching." To his production man he says, "Do some producing." He directs his personnel manager to "do some personneling." As long as these managers do *anything*—good, bad, or indifferent—the president is getting things done through people. But are these the things he wants to get done? Obviously not!

This, then, is the crux of the major weakness in the popular definition of management; that is, results can be good, bad, or indifferent, and the definition of managing will still be met.

Running Versus Managing

The inadequacy of the traditional definition of management is well illustrated by the difference between running an organization and managing an organization. Those who run an organization are often characterized as being extremely busy and working long hours, *hoping* something will happen. In contrast, those who manage *cause* something desirable to happen by first determining what and how something should be done. The sales department that concentrates on getting rid of what it has is being *run*. That sales department is being *managed* when it first determines *what* it should sell and *how* it should be sold.

Much to be guarded against is the tendency for insecure and/or incompetent managers to seek solace in activity. The busier they stay and the more activities they initiate and maintain, the more comfortable they feel. Many of these managers, when they are told or surmise that they are not working up to par, will immediately plunge into a raft of additional activities. They may be busier, but they are not more effective. They are *running* rather than managing.

Implicit in any definition of management should be the requirement to cause desirable things to happen. Managers cause desired ends to happen by establishing objectives, directing the attainment of these objectives, and measuring the results.

Positive Results

A better definition is demanded, one that places positive emphasis on the manager's accountability for positive results and a high premium on increasingly favorable results. The definition must emphasize the priority of managerial efforts and the paybacks or returns on these efforts. Peter Drucker's excellent definition meets these requirements. In answering the question, "What is the manager's job," he says:

It is to direct the resources and the efforts of the business toward opportunities for economically significant results. This sounds trite—and it is. But every analysis of actual allocation of resources and efforts in business that I have ever seen or made showed

3

clearly that the bulk of time, work, attention, and money first goes to "problems" rather than to opportunities, and secondly, to areas where even extraordinarily successful performance will have minimal impact on results.[1]

It is not enough for the manager himself to work on the highest priority matters with the greatest return to his organization. He must insist, demand, that those to whom he delegates follow the same approach—that their efforts be directed to the real needs and benefits of the company. Dissipated or misguided efforts are wasteful and should be avoided like a plague. Drucker zeroes in on the potentially large area of wasted effort when he states:

> Business enterprise is not a phenomenon of nature, but one of society. In a social situation, however, events are not distributed according to the "normal distribution" of a natural universe (that is, they are not distributed according to the U-shaped Gaussian curve). In a social situation a very small number of events—10 to 20 percent at most—account for 90 percent of all results whereas the great majority of events account for 10 percent or less of the results.
>
> This is true in the marketplace. A handful of customers out of many thousands produce the bulk of the orders; a handful of products out of hundreds of items in the line produce the bulk of the volume; and so on. This is true of markets, end uses, and distributive channels. It is equally true of sales efforts: a few salesmen, out of several hundred, always produce two-thirds or more of all new business. It is true in the plant: a handful of production runs account for most of the tonnage. It is true of research: a few men in the laboratory produce all the important innovations, as a rule.
>
> It also holds true for practically all personnel "problems": the great bulk of the grievances always come from a few places or from one group of employees (for example, from the older, unmarried women or from the clean-up men on the night shift), as does the great bulk of absenteeism, of turnover, of suggestions under a suggestion system, and of accidents. As studies at the New York

[1] Peter F. Drucker, "Managing for Business Effectiveness," *Harvard Business Review* (May–June 1963), pp. 18–26.

Telephone Company have shown, this is true even in respect to employee sickness.

The importance of this simple statement about "normal distribution" has been grasped by all too few businessmen. It means, first: while 90 percent of the results are being produced by the first 10 percent of events, 90 percent of the costs are being incurred by the remaining and resultless 90 percent of events.

In other words, costs, too, are a "social phenomenon." If we put it into mathematical language, we see that the "normal distribution curve" of business events is a hyperbole with the results plotted along the plus half, and the costs along the minus half of the curve. Thus, results and costs stand in inverse relationship to each other.

And now, translated back into common language, economic results are, by and large, directly proportionate to revenue, while costs are directly proportionate to number of transactions. The only exceptions to this are the purchased materials and parts that go directly into the final product.

For example:

To get a $50,000 order costs no more, as a rule, than to get a $500 order; certainly it does not cost 100 times as much.

To design a new product that does not sell is as expensive as to design a "winner."

It costs just as much to do the paper work for a small order as for a large one—the same order entry, production order, scheduling, billing, collecting, and so on.

It even costs just as much, as a rule, to actually make the product, to package it, and to transport it for a small order as for a large one. Even labor is a "fixed" cost today over any period of time in most manufacturing industries (and in all services) rather than a cost fluctuating with volume. Only purchased materials and parts are truly "variable" costs.[2]

Delegating for Ineffectiveness

A brief review of the actions of one large company reveals how this wasted effort can take place. This company, with annual sales of over $500 million, gradually became

[2] Ibid., p. 22.

cash-rich as it continued to master the profitability of its then-existing product lines. As cash began to build up, management decided to diversify, via acquisitions, into other product lines. The decision was made partly because management believed it made good business sense and partly because of increasing pressures from shareholders and investment analysts to put the idle cash to work. One promising acquisition management considered was an extremely able company with sales and profits only slightly less than its own company. There were many natural advantages in combining the two companies—complementary product lines, common marketing and distribution channels, and almost complete adaptability of management.

The candidate company was rejected because management didn't want to confine its acquisitions to just one large company; if it bought this company it wouldn't be able to afford other acquisitions in the immediate future. Instead, in rapid succession, it acquired a half dozen very small companies with annual sales ranging from $2 million to $41 million. As is usually true, these small companies were headed by their founders, who became millionaires overnight from the proceeds of selling their companies. Several of them retired or left for other pastures. This, coupled with attempts to integrate the smaller companies into the larger company's management practices, created mass havoc among the larger company's management group.

Almost every officer and department head at the company's headquarters soon became heavily enmeshed in trying to assimilate the small companies. Countless long hours and frustrations followed. The parent company's group vice president, who had played a key role in the earlier revitalization of the parent company, spent most of his time on airplanes running from one newly acquired company to another putting out the fires that had not been anticipated at the time of the acquisitions. He was left with little time to devote to the parent company. The controller of the parent company spent almost as much time on the road endeavoring to master the financial intricacies of the new operations. He, too, was left with scant time for his more important role. Another key executive, the corporate director of planning, also spent considerable sums on air fares as he tried to assist the managers of acquired companies to select the better direction for the future and establish even the most rudimentary objectives. The staffs of all three executives worked equally hard.

All three key executives of the parent company provide vivid evidence of what transpires when delegation takes place from a base of misguided direction. Before misdirecting its efforts in the form of the several acquisitions, the company was realizing about $35 million in pretax profits on an investment of about $350 million, or a return on investment of approximately 10 percent. Three years later, with a total investment of $500 million, the company's pretax profits averaged about $15 million, or a decrease in return on investment to about 3 percent.

This company learned the hard way that often it is easier to manage a $500 million company than a $15 million one. The problems are the same but the payback on effort expended is infinitely greater in the larger company. Six years later, after countless months of management talent were spent, only one of the six acquired companies shows any indication of meeting normally expected returns on the time and money invested in it. Even worse, the profitability of the company's main product lines has nosedived. Acquiring the hodgepodge of small companies in lieu of the larger, well-run company put management in the paradoxical position in which the greater the effort and money it expends, the smaller the return. Clearly, management failed to evaluate the priority of its efforts and paybacks properly. There was no dearth of delegation—every officer in the parent company was delegated at least some accountability for the new subsidiaries. Unfortunately for this company, the delegation was made in areas in which the company should not have been involved in the first instance.

The Hierarchy of Wasted Effort

Thus we arrive at one of the major premises on which this book is based, that there is a vast difference between delegation and effective delegation. The adjective "effective" is an all-important one, signifying delegation in a manner that optimizes results. It means that all delegation must be preceded by an exhaustive determination of what is really important to the organization. No matter how religiously all the rules of delegation are followed, they will accomplish nothing if they are not carried out within this framework. Whenever this premise is violated, we will be delegating for ineffectiveness.

Figure 1-1 illustrates the consequences of delegating from top to bottom without regard to priority of efforts. The accelerating impact of the failure of top management to establish proper priorities and direction prior to delegating

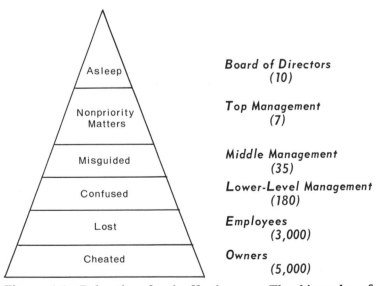

Figure 1-1. Delegating for ineffectiveness: The hierarchy of wasted effort.

to lower levels is shown. The seven top managers delegate to achieve the wrong results, and their action has an impact on the 8,232 persons directly connected to the company.

The more adept management is at delegating, the more the problem of the wrong priority will be compounded, because delegation lines up all efforts to achieve the established priority. A good case might be built in favor of poor delegation when the wrong priority has been established, because this priority won't be achieved so efficiently if the delegation is poor.

To avoid delegating for ineffectiveness, managers must first make basic decisions with respect to:

1. What really needs to be done and what the relative priority of each major objective that needs to be achieved is.

2. What doesn't need to be done. Actions for which there is no real need should be eliminated but never delegated.

The consequences of misdirection—compounded by multilevel delegation—are more serious at the top level, but are by no means confined to this level. They can be disastrous no matter where delegation takes place if priorities and proper direction have not been established first. Consider, for example, a controller who feels that his raison d'être is to maintain accounting records and to issue various reports based on the records. He will delegate to his managers and employees jobs that reflect recordkeeping and report issuing. Another controller regards the records and reports as only a means of accomplishing his primary objective—helping to improve profitability. He looks at the ends, not the means, and delegates profit-generating accountabilities to his people.

The maintenance engineering manager who does "too good" a job and overmaintains machinery and equipment is also ineffective. He insists that everything be maintained in 100 percent perfect order. His costly, misplaced emphasis on unrealistic standards causes his people to increase maintenance costs completely out of proportion to return as the delegation proceeds down the line.

Equally guilty of using assets improperly is the personnel manager who equates the best personnel relations program with the number of different programs he succeeds in getting into operation, regardless of whether or not they serve a real need. He will hold the personnel people below him accountable for fostering the needless programs. Finally, a foreman who pushes his people to lower costs to such an extent that product quality and customer acceptance suffer is pursuing the wrong priorities.

Thus, no matter how skilled and effective the actual delegation is, it will be inimical to the organization's best interests if it results in delegating for ineffectiveness.

Balanced Management

The most effective manager views management as an integrated system much like an integrated production line or integrated plant. If one block in an integrated plant is removed, there is no plant. If there is a weak, or nonfunctioning, phase in an integrated production line, output of the whole production line suffers. Much the same is true of the management process. A man who deserves a top grade on his planning and controlling abilities is a weak manager if he is not able to delegate or get the required results from his subordinates. The man whose technical knowledge is unimpeachable is a poor manager if he cannot translate this knowledge into practice. A high-speed filing, labeling, and packaging line that runs at 125 percent of rated capacity accomplishes little if the labels are put on upside down. The company with a top-quality product and an insatiable customer demand for that product will go nowhere if its personnel and labor relations practices are so poor that it cannot attract and retain employees and it is constantly plagued by work stoppages, strikes, and employee unrest in general.

Similarly, the manager who is an expert in all phases of the management process except delegation must fail. Most of what he accomplishes is through the efforts of his subordinates; he can do very little himself. His outstanding expertise in all other phases of the management process are worth very little if he does not know how to delegate to his subordinates or refuses to do so.

Redefining Delegation

Armed with the revised definition of management that places managers under a solid mandate to accomplish more than just "some thing or things," we can arrive at means for achieving hard-hitting, no-nonsense delegation.

The remainder of this book will discuss delegation in light of the following definition:

> *Delegation is the achievement by a manager of definite, specified results, results previously determined on the basis of a priority of needs, by empowering and motivating subordinates to accomplish all or part of the specific results for which the manager has final accountability. The specific results for which the subordinates are accountable are clearly delineated in advance in terms of output required and time allowed and the subordinates' progress is monitored continuously during the time period.*

There may be those who would fault this definition as merely spelling out in detail that which was implied in the original definition of "getting things done through others." However, I believe that such assumptions have caused considerable misunderstanding and loss in managerial effectiveness. Also, close observation of many managers in action leads me to the conclusion that if such an assumption was made in theory it often was not translated into practice. A definition should be specific and should not require making key assumptions to understand it. However, rather than debating the virtues of any one definition, I want to provide a working definition for the purpose of generating a more

11

constructive discussion of ways and means of improving delegation practices.

Thus, the revised definition of delegation comprises several key components:

1. The determination of priorities
2. The translation of the priorities into objectives or results for the organizational unit
3. The breaking down of the organizational objectives into smaller units to be clearly delegated to managers
4. The establishment of a feedback system to monitor the effectiveness of the delegation

For example, one organization established its priorities for 1974. The president of the company made his top sales manager accountable for the sale of 50,000 units during the calendar year 1974. He in turn delegated part of his accountability to each of the three sales managers reporting to him. Sales manager A became accountable for selling 20,000 units and sales managers B and C for 15,000 units each.

The top sales executive continues to be accountable to the president for selling each and every one of the 50,000 units. However, he has broken up his job into smaller, more manageable, and more controllable parts through delegation to his subordinates. Just as the president is holding the top sales executive accountable for the total number of units sold, the sales executive in turn holds his subordinate managers accountable for their assigned share of his workload. Periodically as the year unfolds, he will monitor the progress of each of his subordinates and take any remedial action called for. He will also conduct a final evaluation at the close of the year.

Elements of Delegation

What are some major elements of delegation required to meet the revised definition? What should we look for as evidence of the amount of delegation that has taken place? In-depth delegation takes place when the manager is given the widest possible latitude to determine his own destiny in the following areas:

Responsibility: jurisdiction or scope of his job

Accountability: specific results he must achieve

Planning: doing the planning for his own organizational unit

Authority: having the authority necessary to make the decisions and take the action appropriate to his job

Decision making: making the decisions that need to be made for his unit

Directing: within a minimal monitoring or control system, being left alone to direct and manage his own organization and its resources

Monitoring: receiving the tailor-made feedback and data necessary to plan for his operation, monitor its progress, and take corrective action as required

Final or Delegated Accountability?

One concept of accountability preached extensively is the concept of final accountability. Traditionalists in management thinking have long asserted that final accountability cannot be delegated, and that the top manager must always shoulder the blame for anything done by his subordinates. On the surface this point is difficult to dispute. However, if we go back far enough the president of a corporation with 50,000 employees becomes ultimately responsible for the actions of every employee, making this concept impractical.

I am concerned with delegated accountabilities, not with preserving or furthering a debate on whether or not final accountability may be delegated. Final accountability smacks too much of a one-man profit-and-loss center, namely, the chief executive officer. Delegated accountability contemplates multiple levels of accountability being carried out by all the managers in an organization.

13

Let's look at a company that has 50 managers at various levels. Assume each manager has an average of five objectives for a particular target period. According to the advocates of final accountability, the president must have 250 objectives—the sum total of all the objectives of all his managers. The typical president would rightfully call such a situation ridiculous.

As a practical matter it seems more appropriate to hold an individual manager accountable for a particular result. In lieu of using the term "final accountability"—fraught as it is with years of debate and misunderstanding—I prefer the term "prime accountability," my own, highly personal description of the specific results the superior expects of the subordinate. Assuming that in-depth delegation has taken place, each of the 50 managers in an organization will have prime accountabilities. Thus the manager who has the "prime accountability" for a result is the manager who must accomplish the result, the doer. His boss—the manager with final accountability—insures that the delegation is carried out, but he doesn't actually "do it." The manager with prime accountability is the key to delegation.

The following abbreviated instructions were given by a corporate president to one of his vice presidents who was being delegated the responsibility for the company's production function:

You've accepted my offer to head our production function. From now on you're in charge. You and I will agree on the results I expect from you, and we'll design a feedback system so both of us will know how well you're performing. We'll agree on your authority and revise it as it becomes necessary. From now on any production problem is your problem, not mine. You'll do the planning for your function; I won't. Any worrying in connection with production will be done by you, not by me. I'll expect you to come to me when you have major problems. I'll expect recommendations, not merely the presentation of problems. The success or failure of the production department will be yours, not mine. The better you do, the better I'll look, but you're now accountable for production. I'm not.

Nonpermissive Management

Delegation does not countenance the form of managerial malpractice often referred to as permissive management. Permissive management may be defined as permitting subordinates to do what they wish whenever they wish. It is incongruous to use the word "management" in the same context. Permissiveness is not managing—it's a good first step to organizational suicide. Permissiveness involves permitting subordinates to "do their own thing" without regard to the priorities and objectives of their units and of the organization as a total entity. Delegation does contemplate granting subordinates the greatest possible voice in determining their jobs and future; always, however, within the overriding requirements of what the organization requires to remain healthy over the long pull.

No-nonsense delegation is delegation *by objectives* and *for* results. It requires two absolute prerequisites if it is to cause things to happen: first, that the organization arrive at valid conclusions concerning its priorities and the objectives it must achieve to carry out these priorities; and second, that delegation be pursued in a manner that permits and requires each manager to play his proper role in achieving the necessary objectives. Managerial effectiveness will suffer if either prerequisite is ignored, doesn't contribute its proportionate share, or is pursued in inverse order.

[2]

WHY DELEGATE?

THOSE UNINITIATED in delegation and those who have never succeeded in practicing it might well question the need for so much emphasis on delegation and the reasons delegation is usually reputed to be so important. There are primary reasons delegation must be practiced if management is to progress and other reasons which, while possibly not as vital, greatly assist the manager in carrying out his role.

Primary Reasons

The major aspects of a manager's job usually are regarded as being composed of planning, organizing, directing, and controlling. They also include evaluating (appraising), compensating, and coaching and developing his people. If the manager is to carry out these responsibilities efficiently, it is absolutely essential that he be skilled in delegation. We will now examine the importance of several

16

major aspects of the manager's job in light of the part delegation plays.

Too often whether or not to delegate is considered a personal choice on the part of each individual manager. In point of fact, there is no choice. If he is to be a true manager he must delegate.

Planning

No manager, regardless of how competent he may be, can plan in detail for all the operations and people in his organizational unit. Each subunit manager must plan for his own group. The manager at the lower level is the expert on his unit; he is more familiar with his operations and people, the special circumstances that may exist at any given point in time, the advantages and disadvantages that should be exploited or minimized, the technical aspects of the operation, and the future potential of his operation. All of these are vital ingredients to profit planning.

Almost invariably plans fail when they are developed by higher level managers for a lower level manager's operations. Study after study and experience after experience have proven that managers are more highly motivated to realize goals when they have played a predominant part in drawing up the original plans. Profit planning achieves its maximum results when each manager regards the plan for his unit as his exclusive plan—one for which he alone is accountable. He will not feel this way if the plan is foisted upon him by his boss. Similarly, he will be quite reluctant to revise his plans and objectives downward as the target period unfolds if they are truly his plans and objectives. He will not experience this reluctance if he merely is administering someone else's plan. Why should he? It wasn't his plan in the first place. Why should he care what someone else does to "their" plan? Thus, without delegation for planning, the two most important aspects of profit planning—the drives to develop effective plans in the first instance and to be com-

17

pletely unwilling to lower objectives unless absolutely necessary—are lost.

Many organizations learned this the hard way with the advent of establishing the job of director of planning at headquarters level. Initially, these new staff managers tried to do all the planning for the organization. The plans looked great on paper and met all the principles of planning, but they just didn't work out in practice. Industry soon moved the planning function back to each individual manager and started using the planning manager as a coordinator and coach on the techniques of planning.

Controlling

Managers, especially senior managers, often wonder why so many things seem to go wrong before they know about them and have an opportunity to take preventive action. They wonder why their controls, particularly those with supposedly built-in early warning signals, aren't alerting them to many of these problems in advance.

Much of the answer would appear to be obvious. Control implies that each major function to be performed in an organization has been clearly assigned to a specific individual and that the individual's accountability has been clearly fixed in terms of what he must accomplish. Controls cannot be effective if this has not been done. How, for example, can control be established over the operations of a key divisional sales manager when the vice president of sales has never delegated any accountability for results to the divisional manager?

The problem is illustrated by the case of the company engaged in selling and servicing property and casualty insurance. The sales department is headed by a sales vice president. The United States is divided into four sales divisions, each headed by a sales division manager who reports to the sales vice president.

Each of the sales divisions has in it several large-volume

customers, who account for sizable portions of business. These large-volume customers are known as key accounts. When a major problem occurs with a key account, the sales vice president often steps in and deals directly with the customer. On other occasions, he will review the problem with the appropriate sales division manager and have the latter deal with the customer to settle the problem. There is no apparent pattern to when the vice president will handle problems himself or delegate to others. There is a legitimate question as to whether the vice president or the division manager is accountable for key account sales and customer service. The question concerning accountability raises questions concerning the control. Should the control be tailored to measure the vice president's actions or those of the division manager? Which one should take the initiative in acting on the reports that flow from the controls? Should the controls attempt the undesirable end of measuring the joint performance of both managers?

Control implies standards, measurements, and reporting or sensing systems. The standard being sought (the delegated accountability) must be stated as definitely as possible. The measurement then is applied to the standard. The resulting comparison serves as the basis for the reporting system. When the standard is nebulous it logically follows that the next two steps in the sequence—measuring and reporting—will suffer accordingly.

General controls or controls over general accountabilities are ineffective, confusing, and misleading. Therefore, controls must be preceded by a delegation that is specific as to exactly who is accountable for exactly what. Effective, purposeful controls are described in detail in Chapter 12.

Evaluating Managers

Meaningful evaluation cannot take place without delegation. Violation of this truism has a far-reaching impact on an organization because so much of the organization's future hinges on the validity of the evaluation procedure. It should aid in distinguishing between the outstanding, the average, and the weak performer. It should serve as the primary basis for making promotions and demotions, for compensating managers, and for helping to determine training and development needs for each manager. In short, if the quality of a company's managers determines the future of the organization—and few would disagree that it does—the quality should be based on the best possible evaluation techniques.

Yet some of the most prevalent prostitution of the management process has taken place in the form of endeavoring to evaluate managers without first delegating to them. It has been only during the past few years that a minority of companies has been willing to depart from 50 years of malpractice and begin evaluating what managers have achieved on the basis of what they were delegated the responsibility and means to accomplish. The vast majority of organizations continue to practice "cowpath" management by following the majority and evaluating their managers on the basis of nonresults-oriented personality traits. It is impossible to evaluate a quality control director's performance when his responsibility is spelled out in vague descriptions such as "to recommend and administer a quality control program designed to assure that the company's products are of the highest quality." This vague description of what was delegated to one manager is in marked contrast to the accountability delegated to a data processing manager who was required "to decrease from ten to five days the amount of time required to distribute the monthly report of operations, without an increase in total costs." Specific accountability has been delegated to the data processing manager and his performance can be evaluated quite accurately. Chapter 15 covers evaluation in considerable depth.

Compensation

Regardless of the form it may take—salary, incentive payments, stock options—managers should be compensated on the basis of and in proportion to the results they achieve. Too often, however, compensation takes the form of rather uniform "handouts" based on such criteria as the highly subjective thinking of senior managers.

Compensation experts have preached for years that the two all-important objectives of all compensation plans must be to motivate managers and to provide equity. Neither objective is served unless delegation has taken place first. Equitable compensation is a highly individual matter and must be tied directly to how well the manager has achieved his delegated objectives. We should not merely tell a sales manager to go out and sell; this delegation is too vague to constitute a proper basis for compensating him later. How would he be evaluated if he sold 10 units, 20 units, or 100 units? What should he have sold during the period? As he wasn't delegated any specific accountability it is impossible to evaluate how well he performed or how much compensation he should receive for his efforts. He'll probably receive what his boss subjectively believes he should be paid. However, if he had been made accountable for the sale of 40 units at a unit price of $12,000 during the period, a proper base would have been established for both evaluating and compensating him and the objectives of equitable compensation would have been served. Once again, delegation becomes a key to another vital aspect of the management function.

Development of Subordinates

Chapter 14 is devoted to developing subordinates through delegation. Development is mentioned briefly here to acknowledge its status as one of the primary reasons managers must delegate. No other part of the manager's job is more important than his mandate for helping to develop his subordinates. His top chore in this regard is to provide them with the opportunity and tools for developing themselves. Subordinates who don't develop have already been where they are going and the result is a static or regressive organization. If development were something a manager could "do" to his subordinate, delegation might not be necessary to the subordinate's development. However, development is something a subordinate must do for himself, and prior delegation is the vital ingredient.

A fledgling flyer doesn't master flying by sitting beside the pilot and observing him. The student may learn some of the principles of keeping the plane aloft but he'll never learn how to fly until his instructor lets him solo—until the student is delegated the definite accountability for the takeoff, flight, and landing.

As a corollary, the instructor (the boss) will never know if his subordinate (the student pilot) can execute the accountability of a pilot until he is delegated this actual assignment. Delegation to the student pilot also provides the instructor with the basis for evaluating the student as a poor, fair, or excellent pilot. This evaluation provides the instructor with a basis for determining what additional training the student will require, and could not have been made prior to the actual delegation. The same reasoning applies to developing a manager. His development and competence will not be complete until he is delegated definite accountability he alone must handle, is given the necessary authority, and is left alone to carry it out.

Secondary Reasons

The preceding sections discussed several aspects of the manager's job for which delegation is an absolute prerequisite to successful accomplishment. The following sections highlight additional reasons managers should delegate.

Utilization of Assets

The manager who refuses to delegate is not unlike the person who has considerable money but refuses to use it even to earn interest. The wise manager delegates as much as his people can handle; in doing so he maximizes the return on the people investment with which his organization has entrusted him. Examples of two contrasting managers will illustrate this point.

Manager A has six managers reporting to him. Instead of delegating a part of his job to each of them, he refuses to delegate and tries, unsuccessfully, to do everything himself. The six subordinate managers are denied the opportunity to make a contribution or are only allowed to make a contribution far below their potential. Manager A's actions indicate he believes that he can accomplish more acting alone than his total group of seven managers (himself and his six subordinates) acting as a coordinated whole.

Manager B is the opposite. He operates under the premise that each of his six managers has unique talents and abilities he doesn't have. He delegates definite accountability to each manager for a part of the total operation. The combined contributions of this group will be infinitely greater than the group headed by manager A and the return on the company's investment in its managers will be commensurately higher. Manager A is like the pilot who tries to get top speed from his airplane while running only two of its four engines. Manager B uses all four engines and makes certain that each is carrying its proper share of the load; he will travel faster and farther in the same amount of time.

Self-Direction and Motivation

Probably few things are as frustrating to a competent manager as the need to look over the shoulder of a subordinate constantly. Is he doing his job? Is he doing it right? Is he doing enough? Is he doing it on schedule? The frustration experienced by the subordinate more than matches that of his boss. He considers himself hounded, picked on, and a failure in the eyes of his boss. It is small wonder that he becomes increasingly disinterested in doing more and doing it better as his confidence in himself continues to erode.

23

An effective manager endeavors to avoid this self-defeating mode of operation by making the subordinate act as his own boss wherever and whenever possible and prudent. He delegates definite accountability to his people and holds them strictly accountable for the final result. By doing so he transfers much of the "monkey" for supervising the day-to-day projects from his own back to those of his subordinates. If he has delegated properly and to the right person, the subordinate himself will handle the detailed checking and the boss will become involved only during the previously established progress review sessions. In effect, the subordinate acts as president of his own little company. Unless he is one of a small percentage of incompetent or untrustworthy employees, the subordinate will do everything possible to make his little company a success. Case after case has proven this premise until it has become almost a truism. Invariably, when a competent manager is given this type of delegated accountability, his productivity, the return to his organization, and his own job satisfaction all overshadow that of a manager to whom delegation has never been made. The latter is oversupervised and overcontrolled, and becomes overly frustrated and dissatisfied. His superior makes it more difficult for himself and those reporting to him. Increased delegation spawns increased self-direction by managers and will go far toward increasing managerial productivity in an era in which the need for it is at a premium.

Foreign Operations

The greater the number of foreign operations, the greater the need for delegation. In addition to the increased need for delegation resulting from the geographical distances involved (covered in another section of this chapter) other major differences in each country must be taken into consideration. Each emphasizes the need for delegation to the managers who represent the organization in the country involved. Some major differences are fringe benefits and allowances (marriage allowances in Japan and excessively high severance pay in Latin America); the laws that require hiring a certain percentage of local nationals (in Latin America and certain European countries); protection against currency fluctuations (in all countries typified by unstable currencies); repatriation of earnings (in many countries); and local customs and practices (in all countries). These differences mitigate against any attempt to hoard all authority and accountability in one central location, such as corporate headquarters. Although it is possible and desirable to promulgate overall policies and objectives, the operating decisions must be delegated to the man on the spot.

One large U.S. corporation recently acquired a major interest in a Japanese company. Prior to being able to work out the necessary delegation, the manager on location in Tokyo forwarded a telegram outlining his plan to grant a "marriage payment" to a key employee who was getting married. The manager's superior in the United States wired back disapproving the payment. He said the company wasn't in the business of subsidizing marriages or the children that might follow the marriage, not knowing that such marriage payments are a way of life in Japan. Considerable dissatisfaction among the Japanese employees resulted before the main office became aware of the custom and reversed itself. The local manager, operating with top policy guidance and with delegated authority, could have prevented this situation.

Professional Managers

The greater the number of professional managers in an organization, the greater the need for delegation to their subordinates. Usually the professional manager has not grown up in the organization he manages and is therefore not familiar with its details. More so than nonprofessional managers, his job is one of managing and getting results. He is skilled at transferring his managerial abilities from one or-

25

ganization to another regardless of the differing product lines and circumstances. Even if it were desirable to gain an intimate, detailed knowledge of operations, he could not hope to do so. He is forced to rely on others; he is forced to delegate. The main emphasis in his job, more so than other managers, must be on becoming a skilled delegator. He must be adept at determining the overall priorities and direction for the company, assisting his managers in setting their objectives, and establishing and utilizing controls designed to measure the performance of his managers and to alert him, in advance, to major problems as they may develop.

The transition from a nonprofessional to a professional manager is not an easy one to master and many who strive to make it never succeed, as evidenced by the following example. After a long career in one company an extremely successful high ranking officer resigned to become president of a large multidivision, geographically dispersed company. He relied heavily on his management skills being transferable from the first company to the second. However, his consuming drive to do a perfect job in the second company led to his downfall. Driving himself to the point of exhaustion, he immersed himself deeply into every phase and detail of the company. He had an excessive number of people reporting to him under a misguided attempt to keep on top of everything. He demanded that all data be triple-checked before a decision was made. Delegation suffered, authority became highly centralized in geographically decentralized operations, decision making slowed to a snail's pace, and the new president was soon removed.

Distance

The greater the distance between an operation and the person to whom it reports, the greater the need for delegation to the manager on the spot. Even with the dramatic advances in the speed and content of communications transmission and the speed of travel accompanying the jet age, a tremendous potential loss exists when the local manager is not empowered to act.

One company with sizable cash reserves in a foreign country lost over $150,000 in one day from fluctuations in the local currency. The local manager spent almost the entire day telephoning headquarters and sending telegrams trying to outline the situation and get approval to act. While this exercise in futile communications was unraveling, the currency was devalued and the company lost the income, which was equal to $1 million in sales effort.

A local plant manager suffered the same fate in connection with a threatened strike by his unionized employees. He, too, spent hours on the phone outlining the situation and defending his recommendation to grant a particular concession—one he believed to be equitable for both parties. All he got for his efforts was a promise from headquarters that the operations vice president and the company's top labor relations manager would fly to the plant to size up the situation before any offer was made to the union. In the interim the union struck the plant and a costly three-week strike followed. Because of the ill feeling generated by the strike, it was ultimately settled on terms considerably more costly than those proposed originally by the plant manager.

One of the commoner indictments of headquarters by local management is that headquarters doesn't understand the local problems and circumstances. Headquarters is quick to counter that local management doesn't understand "the big picture." Many of the reasons for this differing viewpoint could be lessened through well-coordinated delegation.

Management Capabilities

The higher the capabilities of managers (experience, education, training, technical knowledge, competence), the greater the need to delegate. The need is especially important for this high-talent group because these managers

27

possess the potential for making contributions of a higher order and they become dissatisfied more readily if not given the opportunity to make the contributions they feel they are capable of making.

One long-established chemical-related company had been dominated for years by the president and his father before him. The president correctly sized up the coming boom in certain aspects of the general chemical industry. To gain an immediate position in the business the company quickly acquired a half dozen smaller companies in the industry. These acquired companies were staffed largely by well-educated managers with advanced degrees in the applicable technologies. Each tended to be an individualist bent on making his mark—qualities which had made their smaller companies successful enough to be acquired by the older company.

The president's initial attempt to mold these managers into the rigorously controlled system he had practiced in the past threatened to ruin both the parent company and the acquired entities. An eleventh-hour decision all but forced on the president by his board resulted in each of the acquired companies being given considerable autonomy to manage its own operations. Today, dissatisfaction has gone down to normal levels, the managers have had their individuality and interests restored, and the company's sales and profits are zooming.

Diversity of Products

The more diverse the product or service line, the greater the need for delegation, and the need increases with increases in the quantity or volume of these lines. ITT is an outstanding example. Its product lines run the gamut from bakeries to hotels to rental cars to insurance to communications to intricate electronic hardware. The revenue from each is sizable. Delegation in the form of decentralized operations becomes an absolute requirement for this company in light of the sheer weight of numbers and the many differing complexities involved. The New York headquarters establishes broad overall policies (such as the minimum return required on investment), assists in establishing objectives and plans for each major unit, and then establishes tight controls to continually measure the performance of each unit. Within this framework, with the exception of instances in which major problems develop and headquarters injects itself, the actual operation of each unit is delegated to the unit head.

One has only to imagine the difficulty of trying to operate this far-flung organization on a highly centralized basis to appreciate the futility and chaos that would ensue. How could even the most competent executive be able at one moment to make informed decisions on the production and marketing of bread in the United States, on the intricacies of marketing products in Common Market countries, on the expansion of a rental car franchise to Chillicothe, Ohio, and finally on negotiating a new telecommunications operating contract with the government of Guatemala? The need for effective delegation appears obvious to anyone who has had even brief experience with managing diverse operations.

Larger Organizations

The larger the organization, in terms of the number of employees, managers, and levels of management, the greater the need to delegate. The possibility of "one-man shows" being successful decreases as the size of the entity increases. This should not be interpreted to mean that delegation is of no importance in the smaller organization. It merely means it is of less importance when the unit is smaller. The president of a small company having only one plant and a few hundred employees usually is quite familiar with most aspects of the operation and the need for delegation is not so obvious. However, as his company grows to several plants and to 2,000 or 3,000 employees he is no

29

longer able to maintain his intimate knowledge and must rely on others. Both the volume of work and accompanying decisions that must be made and the additional disciplines and knowledge that accompany the expansion, such as personnel and labor relations, quality control, financial controls, sales and marketing, forecasting, and product development, prevent him from handling everything himself.

One of the challenges faced by a manager at any level is to remain flexible enough to adjust his management style quickly as changes take place in his unit. Among other things he must become more and more skilled at delegating as his unit increases in size and complexity. The manager who continues to run his expanded unit as if it were the small unit of old will find that his management style has changed from successful to unsuccessful.

Ease of Managing

The greater the ease with which a manager chooses to manage, the greater the need for delegating. The manager who chooses to try to do everything with his own two hands will suffer at least three undesirable results. He limits his own productivity, he limits his potential contribution to his organization, and any contribution he does make will be accompanied by frustration and an excessive amount of personal effort. Unfortunately, many managers revel in working long and hard hours and endeavor to do too much themselves, including many things that should be delegated to others. One of the vital tests of an effective manager is how easy, not how difficult, he makes his job. He should seize every opportunity and tool available. Delegation is one of the more important tools. He should measure himself by the results achieved and not by the amount and difficulty of the effort expended. His subordinates can help him make his own job easier and more productive if he knows how to utilize them and makes a concerted effort to permit them to assist him.

Failure to delegate specific authorities and accountabilities to subordinates leaves the superior in the weak position of having no real basis for judging the subordinates' accomplishments and development needs. Rewards like salary increases and promotions tend to be made without any factual basis and are often based on whim and intuition. Planning, to the extent it takes place at all, tends to be more fiction than fact.

Also, the manager who fails to delegate becomes more of a doer than a manager. He works harder under more adverse circumstances and usually accomplishes less than his counterpart who practices delegation at every possible opportunity. Finally, the manager who doesn't delegate is failing to carry out one of the cardinal parts of his job as a manager. He doesn't deserve to be called a manager at all.

[3]

SYMPTOMS OF
POOR DELEGATION

THE DISTANCE between the in- and out-baskets is usually
only about three feet but it can be the largest and most important distance in the world to an organization's future.
The quality of action management takes between these two
baskets, the decisions it makes, and the results they achieve
determine the company's success or failure. Critical to this
action is the amount and quality of delegation that take
place.

Delegation, therefore, entails more than transferring the
contents from one basket to the other. Although this procedure does distribute the work for someone else to perform,
it accomplishes little else. Certainly, no delegation has taken
place. About all that's happened is that a very loose responsibility for the project or activity has been moved from one
physical location to another. Yet if in-basket is changed to
"superior" and out-basket to "subordinate," we find that the
same thing happens every day in management.

32

Unfortunately, those who do the shuffling often believe that they have delegated and that the delegated matters are well in hand and being pursued actively and with vigor. They would be well advised to critically review their organizations for symptoms of poor delegation. It is one thing to chant continuously about the virtues of delegation and to damn those who don't seem to measure up to the delegation. It is eminently more worthwhile to say less and do more to correct the problem.

What to Look Out For

Just as physical symptoms provide the patient and doctor with guidance as to the nature and extent of the patient's illness, symptoms of weak delegation provide the manager with guidance as to the causes and methods of treatment. Good managers treat causes rather than symptoms; hopefully, the symptoms then disappear. This chapter will discuss the commoner symptoms of ineffective delegation as an aid for determining the seriousness of the problem. Chapter 4 will examine the causes and the remaining chapters will offer proven suggestions for treating the problem.

The reader is counseled to evaluate carefully each of the following symptoms of weak delegation to determine whether or not it is in reality truly symptomatic of delegation illnesses in his organization. All of them may not be valid indicators for every organization. However, each is worthy of careful evaluation, as it may well provide the direction for corrective action.

Poor planning. Lack of delegation is second only to untrained planners as the cause of weak planning. Plans that frequently go astray should be considered symptomatic of poor delegation. Frequently the plans are developed at higher levels by misguided executives operating under the false premise that planning can be done only by those who are in a position to see the overall picture. This is unmistakably true when it comes to providing guidance and direction for the organization. However, it fails to recognize that the overall picture consists of smaller pieces and that the manager in charge of the smaller operation knows that operation better than anyone else. More realistic planning invariably results when each manager does his own planning at his level within a larger planning framework and when all the smaller pieces are coordinated into the total picture. Planning is one instance in which too many cooks don't spoil the broth—as long as each knows his part of the recipe.

Frequency of orders. The number of orders issued by the superior and the amount of detail they contain are valid indicators of how much delegation has taken place. The degree can vary from continually issuing detailed standard operating procedures to the subordinate to having him manage under approved objectives with most of the "how to" left to the subordinate's discretion. The vital parts of delegation—discretion, initiative, and decision making—decrease as the frequency and detail of orders increase.

A production superintendent considered himself to be skilled in delegation because his department's productivity was relatively high. He frequently bragged about the authority enjoyed by his general foreman. However, practice did not support his contention. Whenever even the smallest problem developed in the department the superintendent would enter the picture and in rapid-fire succession would state what he believed the problem was, what should be done to correct it, and who should be involved in the corrective action. Thus, whenever a real test occurred, it became clear that little delegation had been made to the general foreman. He was in the position of waiting constantly for frequent and detailed orders.

Overcontrol. Even the best initial delegation can be destroyed by subsequent overcontrol. Symptoms of overcontrol include the daily staff meeting, frequent visits to the subordinate's unit, frequent interoffice telephone calls, requests for an excessive number of reports, a close check required of the financial department on components of the subordinate's operations, and encouragement of the subordinate to run to the superior with bits and snatches of information on his operation.

These actions usually indicate a lack of trust in the subordinate. To the extent they are overdone, they indicate that the superior has not entrusted a portion of his decision-making authority to the subordinate. The subordinate is not likely to accept accountability for results nor will he be too concerned about mistakes causing too much of a problem. He knows that "big brother" is watching and will detect, and probably act, if any mistakes appear on the horizon. The amount of control exerted should be limited to the *minimal* amount required to: (1) Operate as an early warning system that permits remedial action to be taken on major problems while there is still time to take the action. (2) Provide assistance to the subordinate before he gets in over his head on *major* problems.

Undercontrol. Undercontrol is as much a symptom of poor delegation as overcontrol is. It is detrimental to a manager's motivation. He begins to believe that his superiors have no real interest in what he is doing and that his job is not very important to the company. He tends to equate the importance of his job with the amount of interest others show in what he is trying to accomplish. One type of boss stops into the subordinate's office each day and asks how things are going and how the subordinate is doing. Regardless of what answer the subordinate may give, the boss leaves with a comment like "That's good, you handle it." After a certain number of these exchanges, the subordinate is likely to reply equally automatically that everything is great or fine or proceeding smoothly. Why shouldn't he? By now he firmly believes that he is being ignored to the point where it would make little difference if he reported the building was on fire or he was systematically stealing from the company.

Fat briefcases. The bulging briefcase carried home

35

every night and every weekend is a good indication that one or more of these conditions prevails: The manager doesn't have enough people to handle the workload, he is overly cautious when making decisions, he likes to revel in self-praise about his output, he's trying to impress others, or he is a poor delegator. Every manager gets behind occasionally and has to work overtime to catch up. This should be exceptional, however, rather than routine. Unfortunately there is a tendency for managers to follow the leader. When the leader continually works from a fat briefcase, all but the most hardy souls reporting to him will follow the same practice. It's like a standard for the department. The problem then compounds itself as it moves down through the various levels of management.

Constant pressure. Lack of delegation frequently manifests itself in a manager working under constant pressure. He never seems to relax and his day is filled with problems and panic situations. He always seems to be juggling several balls at the same time. When he is able to put down one ball there is another one to take its place. This unenviable situation may have two different causes. The manager's boss has not made an effective delegation to the manager, or the manager has not delegated to his subordinates. In either case, the manager is caught in the middle and he will continue to work under pressure until the weakness in delegation is corrected or until the pressure is removed via the cardiac route.

Criticism of subordinates. The manager who always criticizes his subordinates, both directly and to his superior, probably has a delegation problem. Seldom, if ever, unless it is by design, will a manager end up with all the poor managers in the organization. More often a bad situation is of his own making. He delegates only minimal accountabilities to the people he is criticizing. Then he double-checks them to an excessive degree. He justifies the double-checking by expressing dissatisfaction with his people. His subordinates, even if they are truly substandard, will have a difficult task improving themselves if they are never made responsible for their own actions.

Lack of policy. This is a major indicator of poor delegation. The lack of policy enunciation, communication, and feedback to subordinates can cause a delegation problem by design or by accident. It is by design if the manager hasn't provided it as a means of forcing his subordinates to check with him on all issues. If not by design, the checking back with the boss will take place anyway simply because the subordinates do not have enough information to make a decision. Effective delegation is hampered in either instance.

Too much policy. Conversely, the presence of an overabundance of policies, procedures, and administrative rules also can do violence to delegation. These remove too much discretion from the subordinate's domain and often cause him to be more of a policy administrator than a manager. This is one of the chief reasons private enterprise is often reluctant to place a civil servant in any responsible management position requiring the exercise of independent thinking and judgment preliminary to decision making. Many people with civil service experience are completely lost when a decision is demanded quickly and no policy manual covers the situation.

Lack of objectives. Unless a subordinate operates with clear-cut objectives, he really doesn't know what is expected of him or what he should be doing at any time. He will flounder around and require frequent contacts with his boss to maintain any direction at all. Even worse, he may ignore checking with the boss and do nothing at all until he is criticized or decides to leave for more challenging pastures; this is of critical importance when management jobs are involved. The changes self-direction and self-managing bring about following delegation were discussed in Chapter 2.

Slow decision making. One of the requirements for prompt decision making is that the manager know what he is supposed to accomplish and how much authority he has. A

37

manager who is hazy about his accountability and authority will be equally hazy when a decision is called for. If he makes a decision at all it will be delayed until the last possible moment and the working tempo of all other managers involved in the decision will be slowed down. Avoiding this waste of time is one of the moving factors behind the principle that decisions should be made at the lowest possible level in the organization at which all the information necessary for making the decision comes together. Naturally, locating decision-making authority at the lowest level requires clear, specific delegation. Otherwise the decision-making locus moves up the line to higher levels. There is a high degree of correlation between the extent and clarity of delegation and the level at which a decision is made. An extreme, but actual, example of the impact of this correlation resulted in the decision to switch from one brand of work gloves to another being made by the vice president of production, rather than by the foreman or plant manager, who more properly should have done it.

Misplaced decision making. An outstanding example of a lack of clear-cut delegation leading to decisions being made by the wrong managers frequently took place in a food company in upstate New York. This was not an isolated example. It tended to be the rule rather than an exception. The company's board of directors was an inside board made up of the senior officers in charge of each major function. Over the years the officers had fallen into the habit of calling an informal board meeting whenever a potential "hot chestnut" developed. The issue of the moment was passed around at these meetings until someone, regardless of his functional area, expressed his opinion as to what should be done. The basis of his expertise to render an opinion was seldom questioned; the others usually were content when one of their associates went out on a limb.

Because cost control over manufacturing operations was so poor, the industrial engineer proposed a well-thought-out and much needed standard cost program. As usual, a board meeting was hastily convened and the standard cost issue was started on the well-worn path around the director's table. After it had circumnavigated the table a couple of times, the vice president of sales finally spoke up and demanded the recommendation be rejected because of its possible impact on the morale of plant employees. The others seized on his recommendation and the project was killed.

Thus, the effective decision in this instance was made by the sales executive rather than by the production executive with the counsel of the others involved—finance, personnel, and industrial engineering. This country club atmosphere in which all major decisions were made by a group or by the wrong manager was one of the main reasons the company began to slip. It necessitated a complete management reorganization a couple of years later.

Span of control. Although the number of persons reporting to a manager is not, in itself, a valid indicator as to how much delegation has taken place—a manager could have 25 people reporting to him without giving any of them any authority or accountability—a limited span of control is worth investigating as a possible symptom of poor delegation. Often it indicates a situation in which a manager may be trying to centralize all operations and concentrate power in the hands of a few subordinates. With only a few managers reporting to him, the boss can keep his finger actively in all pies.

Conversely, delegation permits a wider span of control. Probably there is little question but that the limited span of control theory has been perverted by those who refuse to delegate and use it to justify why only three or four people report to them. In many instances it is entirely possible and feasible to have eight or ten people report to a single manager. The manager of the Boston Pops Orchestra has scores of people reporting to him and few would doubt that his is an efficient organization that gets results.

Ball carrying by subordinates. One valid indication of poor delegation is not permitting a subordinate to participate in many meetings and presentations or to make contacts with managers above his own level, even though he has the competence to participate in these relationships.

A manager of wage and salary administration was regarded both within and outside his company as a real expert in his field. However, he reported to a vice president of industrial relations who did not practice effective delegation; he insisted that he would handle any contact with other officers on the subject of wages and salaries. He advocated that "only an officer should talk to other officers." As a minimum, he insisted that he be present whenever the manager of wage and salary administration talked to any of the higher ranking executives. Almost all the presentations made to the board or the operating management committee were made by the vice president. Even when the manager was permitted to participate, his comments were often interrupted, fortified, or explained by the vice president. It became rather obvious in this instance that no delegation had taken place. The vice president in this case probably was motivated at least in part by a desire to keep his company political fences in good shape, but the plain fact is that delegation suffered as a result.

Delegation has not taken place when the person to whom the delegation allegedly has been made doesn't enjoy the freedom to talk to anyone who can help him carry out his delegation.

Spending money. An almost complete lack of delegation commonly becomes apparent when an expenditure of money is involved. A manager may be told he is in complete charge of his operation and should run it as he sees fit. On the surface it appears he has considerable latitude and authority. However, if he must turn to his superior whenever any amount over a few dollars is involved, the manager quickly learns that he doesn't enjoy much authority after all. Any delegation that isn't accompanied by the authority to spend the necessary money to carry it out isn't a very extensive delegation.

Certainly managers should not have unlimited authority to make expenditures. Limits are necessary, but these should be spelled out to the manager and a control established over how well he exercises his authority.

An excellent example and checkpoint is the manner in which a manager is permitted to grant salary increases. Employees look upon the man who grants their salary increases as their true boss. He won't be much of a boss in their eyes if he must secure the concurrence of the personnel department and his superior every time he wants to grant an increase. His authority in this regard as well as in regard to other operating and capital expenditures should be spelled out and given to him when he receives his delegation.

Quoting the boss. The number of times a manager quotes or uses his boss's name to secure action, defer action, or sneak away from making a decision is symptomatic of delegation problems. When any of these occurs, one of three components of delegation has broken down: the manager has not been delegated to, he has not accepted the delegation, or he is not competent to carry out the delegation.

Early in my career I was taught one of my better lessons in delegation by David Dubinsky, then president of the International Ladies Garment Workers' Union. Dubinsky had demanded a sizable concession during collective bargaining negotiations. Momentarily stunned, I replied that I would have to check with my superior before answering the demand in behalf of my company. With a stern and sincere countenance Dubinsky replied, "Young man, you're negotiating this contract. You're the man I'm talking to. If you want to say yes, say yes. If you say yes and don't have the authority to say it, then say it anyway and go back and get your company to support you. If you can't, you're not the man for the job!" Whether I was inclined to say yes or no to Dubinsky, his point was well taken. If you have authority, use it. If you don't, go get it. If you have the authority and don't use it, or if you don't have the authority and can't get it, you're not the man for the job.

41

Detailed job knowledge. A manager, especially one who has several people reporting to him, cannot be expected to know the details of their jobs. If he does, a legitimate question can be raised as to whether he's really acting as a manager or is getting too involved in details of operations. The quick and dirty test here is to ask the manager several detailed questions about the jobs of his subordinates. See if he can answer them or tells you he doesn't know but must check with the man in charge. The manager who can give valid answers every time without checking with his people has delegated in name only. It is suggested that managers like this be complimented for their tremendous grasp of their function and detail and, following this buildup, be told they are not managers but technicians.

Lack of priorities. Another test of the extent to which delegation is practiced is an evaluation of the priorities under which managers are proceeding. Delegation requires establishing priorities. The manager who spends his time—no matter how conscientiously he applies himself—on various matters without regard to the importance of each of them, probably has a delegation problem. Either he has not segregated those unique matters he should reserve for himself from those that should be handled by his subordinate or he has not committed himself to carry out the first requirement of a manager, to maximize the return on the assets entrusted to him.

Everything a secret. Delegation cannot be carried out effectively if there is a lack of communication on matters that affect the delegation. A manager cannot carry out his accountability unless he is provided, on a rather routine need-to-know basis, with all information and data that have an impact on his job. He should not be forced to seek out or request this information; it should flow to him naturally as a part of the system.

Take a shipping foreman whose prime mission is to insure that all shipments are made on time and within allowable cost tolerances. At the very least he must be kept informed of changes in production schedules, changes in delivery dates, agreements made with customers that vary from established policy, projected changes in product and shipping carton design, threatened work stoppages, and the like. They all impact on his operating methods and costs. If these matters are treated as a deep, dark secret by others in the organization, the shipping foreman will not be able to carry out his delegated assignment.

The shipping foreman, in turn, must make certain that he provides ample and effective communications up the line so that his boss will be able to carry out the delegation he has received from his superior. The lack of upward communications often results in the boss becoming isolated and acting on misinformation.

Disorganized effort. Proper delegation should result in a smoothly running team with each manager contributing his necessary input to the total effort. Each manager's contribution is a small cogwheel in the machine. The only way each cogwheel will play its role is to have each manager receive and accept a delegation of what must be done and when it must be done. Otherwise, the team will be replaced by an array of disorganized, uncoordinated individual efforts that mitigate against accomplishing the overall goal. One of the more easily recognized symptoms of poor delegation is a group of heterogeneous managers all going their own way and compounding confusion into a lack of accomplishment.

Critical analysis of symptoms provides guidance as to causes of problems so that remedial action may be taken. Managers who desire to improve their delegation practices and enjoy the benefits are well advised to review each of the following questions and decide whether or not it constitutes a symptom of poor delegation in their organizations.

1. How realistic is my planning? What is the correlation between plans and reality? Why don't plans come true?

2. How frequently and in how much detail do I give orders?

3. Do I overcontrol? Am I limiting my people's actions excessively?

4. Do I undercontrol? Am I ignoring my role as a superior?

5. How much work do I do at home evenings and weekends? How many telephone calls from subordinates do I receive when I'm away from the office?

6. Do I work under constant pressure or only occasional pressure?

7. Am I overly critical of my subordinates?

8. Have I passed on to my people sufficient policy to guide them?

9. Have I severely limited the actions of my people by too many policies?

10. Do my people know my objectives and have they set objectives for themselves? Do mine and theirs complement or contradict each other?

11. Are my people slow or reluctant to make decisions in their assigned areas? Do I have to make too many decisions for them?

12. Are decisions made by the subordinate who should make it or by someone else with my subordinate eager to concur?

13. Have I limited my span of control primarily to keep my finger in all pieces of the pie? Could I gain more by widening the span through effective delegation?

14. Do I permit and encourage my subordinates to participate in meetings and contacts at higher levels when the subject falls in their areas of competence or do I usually try to carry the ball for or with them?

15. Have I given each of my people definite authority to make expenditures?

16. Do I give orders in my boss's name or my own? Which alternative do my people usually follow?

17. Do I try to learn and retain competence in too many details of jobs below me or do I spend almost all my time planning, organizing, directing, and controlling?

18. Do my people and I assign priorities before beginning our tasks or do we treat all tasks as having equal importance?

19. Do my people and I provide each other with the amount and type of information each of us needs to carry out our jobs?

20. Do my people and I function as a team or as a mixture of confused, uncoordinated individuals whose total productivity leaves something to be desired?

[4]

CAUSES OF
POOR DELEGATION

IGNORANCE OF how to delegate has proven, in instance after instance, to be the moving factor behind poor delegation. Doubtless many managers are poor delegators simply because they refuse to delegate; this is one cause of delegation problems. However, most managers do wish to extend their contributions and productivity by delegating. For them, this chapter discusses causes of poor delegation that can be treated through a better understanding of the process. The minority who refuse to delegate are left to divine providence for guidance.

Lack of Understanding

Contrary to the thinking and practice of some managers, delegation involves more than handing out assignments to subordinates. And delegation is not a simple process that can be mastered overnight, subliminally, or by osmosis. Skilled delegators first determine the total content of the process and then make a concerted effort to master it.

One of the commoner errors made by many managers is to conccive of delegation as flowing only from the higher to lower levels; that is, that the superior gives and the subordinate receives. They fail to appreciate that the recipient may not want to accept what is given or that acceptance can vary by many degrees. At the very least, delegation is composed of several major parts, each of which must play its proper role for delegation to be balanced and effective.

An excellent way to get the full import of delegation is to treat it like a legal contract. Just as in a legal contract, the parties (the superior and the subordinate in this instance) to the delegation (the contract) must reach a meeting of the minds as to the content and meaning of the contract's provisions:

1. Agreement on the scope of the job (responsibility)
2. Agreement on the specific results the subordinate is to achieve (accountability)
3. Agreement on the time schedule
4. Agreement on the authority needed to carry out the delegation
5. Agreement on means used to measure performance (control and feedback)
6. Agreement that the superior and subordinate each accepts his part of the contract and will live up to it

Finally, after the contract has been "signed," effective delegation requires that its contents be compared with the contracts of all other managers in the organization to avoid overlapping and duplication of effort, and the delegation contract must be made known to all other managers whose jobs are in any way involved with the manager to whom the delegation was made.

Lack of understanding of the full range of the delegation process often results in omitting one or more critical components. This omission becomes the chief cause of poor delegation on the part of most managers. The next major cause is the failure by either or both parties to carry out the provisions included in the contract. This may result from overreliance on some of the time-honored, but often ineffective and self-defeating, tools of delegation, such as organization charts, job descriptions, and control techniques. Also included in the causes of poor delegation are confusion between the superior and subordinate as to the content of the latter's job, delegation in a vacuum, delegation from an isolated position, and delegation with confused or inadequate authority.

The Slippery Organization Chart

Two of the most popular and most frequently used vehicles on which managers traditionally have based their delegation have been organization charts and job descriptions. They felt that if they gave the subordinate an organization chart portraying his location in the organization, the person to whom he reported, and his relationship to other managers, they had provided him with major guidance as to his job and his delegation. Next they gave the subordinate a lengthy job description to support his position on the organization chart. Now, they reasoned, complete delegation had taken place: the subordinate knew to whom he reported, who reported to him, and what he was supposed to do. These managers, already misguided, sometimes were further misled into believing that the bigger the organization chart in terms of levels and spans of control, the more delegation had taken place.

Figure 4-1 pictures the organization chart of the Old Zapper Insurance Company. An analysis of this chart reveals it to be, with one minor exception which will be discussed later, an excellent example of organization and delegation. The company has been organized to achieve its chief goals of selling and servicing insurance. Next, it has been divided into its major functions: underwriting, claims, legal, finance, and so on. A top manager has been named to head each of these functions. The chart shows what the major functions are and who heads each one. Finally, the chart shows to whom each manager reports. Thus, the chart implies that a

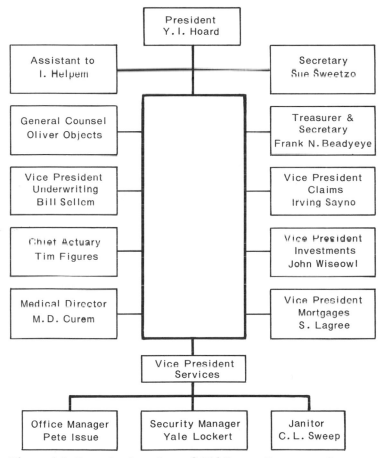

Figure 4-1. Organization chart of Old Zapper Insurance Company showing supposed areas of responsibility.

portion of the total mission of the company has been delegated from the president to each of his managers.

Figure 4-2 dramatizes the minor exception mentioned previously: the organization as it works in actual practice.

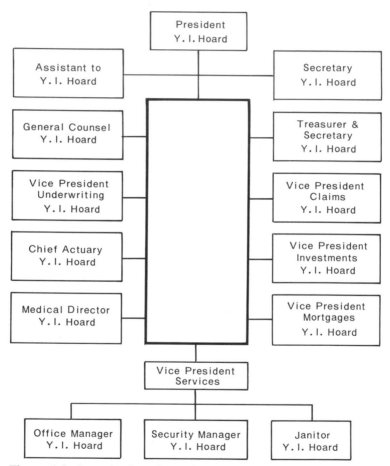

Figure 4-2. Organization chart of Old Zapper Insurance Company showing actual areas of responsibility.

Very little delegation has taken place. In practice, the president calls the shots on all important matters in all departments. The key point here is that an organization chart does not reflect the degree of delegation. In essence, all it does is reflect the job titles that have been assigned and the reporting channels. This exaggerated chart does demonstrate the proven premise that an organization can be pictured in one of three ways: (1) What the company says it is. (2) How it really is. (3) How it should be.

The Nondescriptive Job Description

The typical job description usually is upheld as the prime vehicle of delegation, so it is well to analyze it in considerable detail. Figure 4-3 provides an excellent example of a job description currently in popular use. Many are more than twice this length, but this one will serve for the purposes intended here. It begins with clear-cut data on the job title, the incumbent's name and organizational unit, the job location, the data on which the job description was written, and the person to whom the incumbent reports.

Section I describes the basic function of the job, and section II the nature and scope of the job. The all-important accountabilities are listed in section III. Finally, section IV sets forth critical information such as the division's sales volume, the departmental operating budget, and the number and types of jobs supervised by the incumbent.

The format and content of this job description are the ones most commonly used in industry, in government, and in all other types of organizations. Since the job description is the prime vehicle for delegation, it follows that much of the effectiveness of delegation will hinge on the effectiveness of this job description. We will now analyze the job description in Figure 4-3 in light of its major failings as a tool for delegation.

51

Figure 4-3. Typical job description.

Position: Division Accounting Manager	**Job Code:** Division General
Incumbent: John Doe	**Reports To:** Manager
Organization Unit: Eastern Division	**Location:** New York
Prepared By: JBT	**Date:** January 1, 1966
Approved By:	**Date:**

I BASIC FUNCTION

Under the direction and guidance of the division general manager, manages and coordinates accounting, reporting, and office services activities to assure control over finances and assets of the division.

II NATURE AND SCOPE

This position provides accounting and office management services for the Eastern Division, which includes 6 plants, 10 distribution centers, and 48 branches.

The Accounting and Office Services Department is structured so that a credit manager, a field auditor, an office services supervisor, and about nine clerical personnel report directly to the incumbent. The various activities that the division accounting manager coordinates and supervises are (*a*) credit: determination of credit ratings for customers in Eastern Division; (*b*) field auditing: review of salesmen's records and reports and making judgments on discrepancies; (*c*) accounts receivable: receipt and entry of 5,500 accounts plus miscellaneous receivables; (*d*) merchandise control: analysis and accounting for finished goods; (*e*) sales analysis: analysis of chain sales and billings; (*f*) sales auditing: extension of salesmen's charges and credits; (*g*) cashier: receipt of all cash; (*h*) payroll: preparation of payroll for all nonexempt employees in Eastern Division (sometimes requiring union contract interpretation), six farms, and headquarters research and zone personnel located in New York; (*i*) accounts payable: processes petty cash requests, travel expenses, and miscellaneous invoices through imprest fund; (*j*) discounts and allowances: computation and compilation of salesmen's discounts and allowances; (*k*) switchboard: telephone services for New York office; (l) printing and mail services: printing services to include office forms, production material, and miscellaneous printed matter (labels and headers also printed for Canadian and Southern Divisions).

Coordination of the various accounting activities to result in an accurate and timely measurement of divisional operation is the major objective of this position. To insure that required reports are filed properly and promptly in

Figure 4-3. (Continued).

---

headquarters, the incumbent must influence and depend upon other divisional staff members who are charged with report preparation. In accomplishing this objective, he must be involved continually with the proper selection, supervision, training, and motivation of his assigned personnel.

The division accounting manager advises and assists other divisional staff members in the preparation of the annual profit plan.

The division accounting manager processes applications for the proration of vehicle licenses for the Eastern Division, the Mid-Eastern Division, the Southern Division, and for several vehicles in the Southeastern zone. The proration of vehicle licenses results in tangible dollar savings for the company.

A unique aspect of this position is that portions of various accounting and office management services (credit, payroll, profit planning, printing, vehicle proration) are furnished for other divisions and organizational units of the company. The incumbent is free to operate within established policies and procedures, but the division general manager furnishes direction and guidance in usual problems and reviews progress and results.

III PRINCIPAL ACCOUNTABILITIES

This position is accountable for the following end results:
1. Development and control of effective internal accounting and reporting policies and procedures for divisional locations.
2. Recommendation of improved accounting systems for installation in division.
3. Accurate and timely measurement of results and reporting of divisional operations.
4. Maintenance of the asset records of the division.
5. Selection, training, compensation, and motivation of assigned human resources.
6. Contribution to profit planning through assistance and advice to management staff of Eastern Division.
7. Purchase of office equipment and supplies and provision of miscellaneous office services.

IV DIMENSIONS

Division sales volume (1974 plan) $20,200,000
Departmental operating budget (1974 plan) $ 300,000 (approx.)
Supervision of about 30 employees to include a credit manager, a field auditor, and an office services supervisor

---

Activities, Not Results

Section III, the section that purports to establish the manager's accountabilities, is the critical part of this job description. The entire section is devoid of any specific results (objectives) the incumbent must accomplish. It merely lists the activities in which he should engage until his boss changes the job description. Consider in particular items 4 and 5, which provide that he will maintain the asset records of the division, and select, train, compensate, and motivate the personnel reporting to him. Both of these are excellent examples of activities, not results. The manager will be carrying out his job as long as he maintains records and handles his people. His boss cannot hold him accountable for specific results because none are set forth. The manager cannot be measured on his accomplishments because the description doesn't include any measuring criteria or standards.

At best, his superior can hold him accountable for these two requirements by comparing his performance against the level of generally prevailing and accepted practice in the company and in the industry. What these generally prevailing and acceptable standards are is subject to considerable misunderstanding and varying interpretation between the job incumbent and his boss. These undesirable circumstances could be lessened if the description contained standards against which the manager should be performing.

True accountabilities specify the concrete results to be achieved in a manner that permits measuring such factors as "how much, how well, and when." This job description fails that test.

Changing Priorities

This job description was almost seven years old at the time of this writing. However, the incumbent continued to work under it. Only certain data in section IV were revised to reflect changes in sales volume, budget, and number of employees supervised. The other sections remained basically the same.

Priorities of managerial effort should change with changes in the priorities of the company and the manager's organizational unit. Probably not a single company in existence today has not been forced to change its priorities in the seven years that have passed since this description was written. Yet the job requirements of this particular manager, as reflected by his job description, haven't changed in seven years. How can he follow the same job description year after year and still be supporting the revised priorities of his company? The obvious answer is that he is perpetuating his original activities year after year without regard to priorities except as his duties may be questioned from time to time on a specific issue.

The system doesn't require him to change his priorities, so the job description fails the second test. This is a cruel indictment and it is meant to be. Some readers may counter with the argument that the job description merely establishes the scope of the job followed by the setting of priorities on a day-to-day basis. This is shortsighted management and often indicative of managing on a day-to-day basis. Good management involves planning for the future, hopefully for a minimum of one year. Thus, both the priorities and the manager's major actions should be planned for at least a year in advance. Instead of relying on the premise that the manager's job will change during the year as priorities change, emphasis should be placed whenever possible on determining the priorities and the job in advance. The traditional and often static job description does not place sufficient emphasis on this facet. It relys too heavily on premise and assumption. A more dynamic job description would help insure that the job and priorities proceed hand in hand. When priorities change in the course of carrying out the job, a built-in procedure would facilitate compensatory changes in the manager's actions. In essence, a dynamic description would replace a static one.

Continual Improvement

An organization must insist on continual improvement and plan for it or competition will pass it by or bury it. A worthwhile job description should take this into consideration. This particular one fails the third important test because continual improvement, at least from one year to the next, is not included in a job description that doesn't change for seven years except perhaps in the scope of the job; that is, the manager's job might be decreased or increased by subtracting or adding organizational responsibility. A better description would highlight the need for continual improvement and provide for more explicit measures.

The Man in the Job

Experience has proved that among managers the man makes the job, not the reverse. And the higher the manager proceeds up the line and his authority and responsibilities are broadened, the more he can influence the job. Yet most writers of job descriptions continue to insist that the description ignore the incumbent and concentrate instead on what the company requires of the job. The situation is well illustrated by Figure 4-3, which refers to the scope of the position and the accountabilities of the position. With the possible exception of the outdated and nonmotivating compensation plans widely used today, the job description that purposely ignores the man has been most responsible for the general leveling effect on managerial output.

For example, one job description may cover three production superintendents working on the same job. Each of the managers probably has a different potential and ability to contribute to results but the job description remains the same for all three. It does not address itself to the key issue of different levels of performance from each superintendent. The overriding consideration is the job, not the manager. A better approach is to zero in on the initiative and capability of each manager.

Thus, the fourth failing of the typical job description is its failure to provide the opportunity and encouragement for each manager to contribute according to his own potential, ability, and drive. More workable job descriptions are discussed in Chapter 9.

It would be unfair to condemn all job descriptions on the basis of the weaknesses discussed in the preceding paragraphs. Job descriptions can avoid these weaknesses; many have. There is nothing magical in the form or format of the description an organization uses. The content is what counts and hopefully it will delineate the accountability agreed upon by the superior and subordinate. Once the accountability has been agreed upon and recorded it provides a basis for such related matters as delegating authority and establishing control.

Controls That Don't Control

Inadequate controls follow closely behind organization charts and job descriptions as a contributing cause of poor delegation. Three major categories of control tend to weaken delegation:

1. Trying to apply specific controls to general activities or matters
2. Failing to tailor the control to the accountability it is supposed to measure
3. Emphasizing the costing of products or services, or components of them, over managerial control of operations

Specific Controls

The word "control" itself implies matters of a specific nature. It also implies that managers will be able to use the feedback from the controls to determine how well they are performing and to base the need for taking corrective action. However, in practice, the ability of controls to serve

57

these purposes usually is found wanting. Much of the blame must be attributed to an attempt to apply specific controls to matters of a general nature.

The principal accountabilities spelled out in Figure 4-3 for the division accounting manager are general statements of the activities in which he is required to engage; they are not specific statements of desired results. Consider accountability No. 7 which requires him to purchase equipment and supplies. According to common practice, the control established for this accountability will comprise a review and feedback of the items purchased and their cost. This is not control, but mere bookkeeping. Let's assume the accounting manager purchased 20 items at a total cost of $18,000. The so-called control will dutifully reflect and report on these purchases. Does it control the purchases? It does not. Does it permit corrective action to be taken? It does not. It merely gives a historical picture of the dollar volume of this activity.

The same type of inadequate control is the result whenever they are applied to a job for which accountabilities have not been spelled out as specifically as the controls. Take a sales manager whose specific accountability requires him not only to engage in selling activities, but to sell $100,000 worth of product during the year. His total accountability is broken down by month and by quarter, specifying the dollar volume to be sold during each period. Now controls can be effective. They can measure the sales manager's performance each month by comparing what he sold against what he should have sold. Also, the controls will indicate when corrective action is necessary in order for the manager to carry out his accountability for the year.

Failure to Tailor Controls

No one set of standard controls will serve the needs of all managers in an organization. Each manager will have certain make-or-break factors in his specific operation. For controls to be meaningful and useful, they must be closely tailored to the peculiarities of each manager's operations. Giving each manager the same control report is like letting each one cash a personal check for $1,000 without considering how much he has on deposit in his checking account.

The fallacy of standard control reports is illustrated by two foremen working in the same company. One is in charge of a highly mechanized packaging line in which very expensive packaging materials are involved. The other foreman supervises a labor-intensive utility gang. The first foreman's prime concern will be the capacity of the machine as reflected in machine utilization and quality and cost of the finished product. The second foreman must concentrate on percentage utilization and cost of the men assigned to him. Each must demand and receive control reports that accurately measure their individual make-or-break factors.

Emphasis on Product Costing

The emphasis of too many cost accountants has been on costing out the product or service, or some component of it, instead of on the control the manager requires over his accountability. This premise is substantiated by the wealth of books on cost accounting that dwell almost exclusively on the techniques and methods of calculating costs, allocating costs, and attaining similar information. When mentioned at all, "responsibility accounting"—assisting each manager to control his specific accountability—is treated briefly. Unfortunately, the same disproportionate sense of value is common practice in most companies and other organizations.

The two purposes of cost accounting are not mutually exclusive. The same cost accounting method that is oriented to the control needs of the manager can then be used for product costing. Too often, the initial orientation is to the product and an attempt is made later to adapt the information to serve the manager's control needs. This is much less satisfactory than beginning with the needs of the manager who is intimately involved.

Job Confusion

Effective delegation requires a complete understanding between the manager and his boss as to the content of the manager's job. Yet in-depth research has demonstrated that commonly there is an area of up to 25 percent confusion between what the subordinate believes he is responsible for and what his boss believes he is responsible for. Joe's boss phones him and asks, "Hey, Joe, what the hell happened to costs on No. 2 line?" Joe, equally confused about the inquiry, replies, "How the hell should I know? That's Bill's job, not mine!" Or the president calls in his labor relations director and demands to know why he let the work stoppage occur in Plant 2. The labor relations director explains that he had nothing to do with either permitting or not permitting the work stoppage; the decision was up to the plant manager, a profit center head. Or the financial analyst is called on the carpet because the sales manager is quoting selling prices to customers below the company's established margins. The analyst, ruminating to himself on the stupidity of his boss, replies that he provided accurate cost figures to the sales manager who made the decision. "What else did you want me to do? The sales manager doesn't report to me."

The "what else do you want me to do" question and the confusion it implies must be resolved before delegation can become effective. If confusion exists about job content or accountability, the delegation and the results of the delegation will be similarly confused.

Isolation

The higher the manager is in the hierarchy, the more likely he is to become isolated from the reality of the organization's operations. Once more, the manager faces the old bugaboo of faulty communications. Addressing himself to this problem at the chief executive level, Robert McMurry lists several reasons for the isolation:

1. No subordinate wishes to have his superiors learn of anything which he interprets to be actually or potentially discreditable to him.

2. He learns what his superiors desire to hear. Hence, he becomes adept not only at evaluating the unpleasant but at stressing the positive.

3. Each subordinate is often desirous of impressing the top managers with the superiority of his contributions and, by the same token, of the pitiful inadequacy of the contribution of his rivals.

4. Another source of error arises from the fact that the position of chief executive (and all other managerial jobs) is one for which there is often substantial competition and rivalry.

5. Finally, and from the viewpoint of upward communications of the greatest consequence, there is the inability of many chief executives (and many other managers) to comprehend and accept valid information even when it is brought to their attention.

6. Chief executives (and it's not limited to this level) fail to recognize that for communication to be effective, it must be two way; there has to be a feedback to ascertain the extent to which the message has actually been understood, believed, assimilated, and accepted.[1]

As noted in Chapter 1, managers must delegate for effectiveness. They cannot delegate in this manner if their isolated position precludes them from possessing necessary knowledge on matters such as priorities, problems, and advantages that should be exploited—all key components of the organization atmosphere in which delegation takes place.

Delegation in a Vacuum

A superior cannot delegate to one of his managers without first having considered the job content and account-

[1] Robert N. McMurry, "Clear Communications for Chief Executives," *Harvard Business Review*, March–April 1965, pp. 131–146.

abilities of the other managers in the organization, especially those whose jobs involve matters most comparable to the subject being delegated. An excellent example of the conflict that can arise when delegating in a vacuum occurred in a confection manufacturing company. The manager in charge of the packaging department was delegated accountability for cost improvement to be accomplished by value engineering on all materials being used. At the time this delegation took place, the industrial engineering and purchasing departments already had under way a joint project to accomplish the same end. Considerable ill feeling and wasted effort were generated before the resulting confusion was clarified and the accountability of all three managers was coordinated into concerted action, with each knowing his part in the total project.

In this instance, all three superiors—those in charge of the packaging, industrial engineering, and purchasing departments—were guilty of delegating in a vacuum. To avoid this pitfall, it is necessary to determine what is to be accomplished and then break down the total objective into well-coordinated, individual accountabilities, as illustrated by the next example.

Based on the economic considerations necessary to maximize its return, a company determined the optimum number of units it should sell to be 10,000 during a particular period. The executive vice president, to whom the sales and production departments reported, then proceeded to effect a coordinated delegation between the two departments. In concert with the managers of sales and production, he delegated accountability for matters such as production and inventory levels, purchasing requirements, and sales schedules, levels, and costs. After the delegation had been concluded each manager, including those reporting to the sales and production managers to whom succeeding delegation had been made, knew the part he must play in the combined effort.

Lack of Authority

Lack of authority is both a symptom and a cause of poor delegation. As it is discussed extensively in Chapter 11, it is mentioned here only for continuity and completeness.

The reader might question why the refusal of some managers to delegate is not cited as one of the causes of poor delegation. Refusal to delegate is not a cause of poor delegation. The real causes of refusal are fear and ignorance. The fear is that someone else will make a mistake for which the superior will be held accountable or that the superior will lose power and even security as the subordinate becomes more valuable. Ignorance involves a lack of knowledge on the part of the superior as to how he can multiply his contributions to his company and grow in his job.

[5]

BUILDING
THE FOUNDATION
FOR DELEGATION

DELEGATION IS OFTEN thought of and referred to as a process or a skill. Actually it is a philosophy or a way of life composed of the actual delegation and the atmosphere within which it takes place. Delegation cannot be separated from the management and company atmosphere in which it is carried out. Attempts to do so usually fail because any expertise the manager may demonstrate in the delegation process is offset by conflicting factors in the total atmosphere or context within which the delegation unfolds. The point can be demonstrated by comparing the atmosphere and delegation to a system composed of six highly interrelated components. The system will not operate if any of the components is removed or is not functioning properly. Each component is necessary to successful operation of the total system.

The prerequisites, or components, of the delegation system are:

1. Granting by the superior and accepting by the subordinate of definite accountabilities and an agreement between

the two of the specific results expected, including the means by which results will be measured.

2. Giving enough of the superior's power (authority) to the subordinate to allow him to carry out his accountability.

3. Insuring that there is no overlap or duplication of the subordinate's accountability and authority with that of other managers in the organization.

4. Clearly communicating the delegated accountability to all other managers so that the subordinate can carry out his job with a minimum of confusion and disagreement with other managers.

5. Establishing control or monitoring methods (feedback) by which the progress of the delegation can be gauged from beginning to completion.

6. Establishing the proper management atmosphere.

This chapter will be concerned with the sixth component of the delegation system—management atmosphere—which constitutes the basic foundation on which the other components are built.

Management Styles

Prior to deciding how far delegation can and should proceed in an organization, it is necessary to examine the management style of that organization. Once the style has been identified, the next questions are how much management wishes to change its style and how rapidly it wants to make the change.

The answers to these questions are critical because each style of management rests upon a distinct foundation tailored to that particular style of management. Of the labels often applied to management styles, let's select two—an autocratic style and a participative style of management. Each has its own foundation or "supportive systems," and they are worlds apart. Figure 5-1 illustrates some of the commoner "bricks" in the foundation of a management style.

Under an autocratic style of management each brick in the foundation will have been tailored to support an autocratic structure. Policies will be oriented to centralized decision making, little authority will have been delegated down the line, few managers will participate in actual planning, and feedback will be directed only to the top managers.

In contrast, if a participative style of management is being practiced, policies, planning, decision making, and the like must be characterized by a high degree of decentralization. Delegation requires a generous amount of the participative management style. It is not possible to foist a participative style of management on top of supportive systems designed for an autocratic style, so close attention must be paid to building and maintaining the proper foundation.

The importance of the proper management atmosphere can be illustrated by comparing two common types of managers. One emphasizes control. The other observes the importance of motivation.

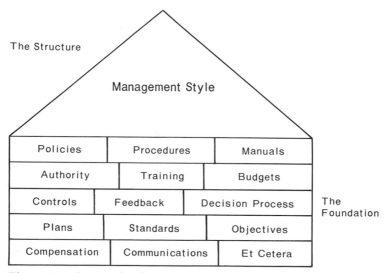

Figure 5-1. Supportive foundation for a management style.

The "Controller"

In this instance, the title does not refer to the financial or accounting manager. It characterizes the manager who regards his primary function as controlling the actions of subordinates. This type of manager is emphasizing the wrong aspect of the management process.

While all managers do have a definite responsibility for controlling or monitoring their operations, control should not be the prime thrust. Those who practice the controller approach to managing usually are guilty of the following:

1. They are more concerned with the hours a man puts in than what the man puts into the hours.
2. They labor with the constant worry that something will go wrong.
3. They dream up and implement all kinds of control devices to keep things from going wrong.
4. They are concerned more with making actual performance match plans than with the level of contribution of the plans.
5. They overdirect, oversupervise, and overcontrol. They control their subordinates rather than develop them.
6. They drive competent subordinates to distraction and to other organizations.

The controller type of manager would be well suited to a full-time, nonmanaging assignment of preparing trial balances—making certain debits and credits agree. In this way, his lack of imagination and delegating ability would not hamper subordinates and the organization.

The Motivator

The motivational approach to managing differs materially from the controller approach. Managers who have a motivational orientation emphasize the following:

1. They are more concerned with a subordinate's accomplishments than with the hours he puts in.
2. They regard control as only a secondary part of their job and exert only the minimum control necessary.
3. They provide subordinates with the maximum opportunity to operate at their highest level of achievement.
4. They emphasize development, not control, of subordinates.
5. Their subordinates enjoy more personal and job satisfaction and, invariably, are more competent than the subordinates of controller-type managers.

How Much Change?

The decision to move from one management style to another cannot be made easily or quickly. A large insurance company in the north-central area of the United States serves as demonstrable evidence of this point. The chief executive officer had heard many complimentary stories about the management-by-objectives system for managing an organization. To operate successfully, management by objectives involves full-scale, in-depth delegation; it is an excellent example of participative management at its best.

The chief executive decided to adopt management by objectives and brought in an outside management consultant for counseling. After talking for two days with the chief executive and his senior officers, the consultant flatly refused to have anything to do with installing MBO in light of the management style and supportive structures then existing in the organization. The company had one of the most puristic autocratic styles the consultant had ever witnessed, and discussions with the senior officers disclosed little evidence of a desire to change it.

Confronted with the consultant's findings, the chief executive was genuinely shocked and stated he was going to change both the style and the supportive systems immediately. Over a period of several months he issued directive after directive, and held meeting after meeting, attempting to accomplish the change. The major change by this president was to bring about almost complete chaos among his managers. They simply weren't geared to such drastic change. Instead of moving immediately to change the management style, he should have first made a determination as to just how much change could and should be made.

How Fast?

Once the determination has been made about how far a management wants to go in changing its style, consideration must be given to how fast the change can be made. The important factors are how fast the supportive systems can be developed to support the new style and how fast the support of key managers can be gained. There are no magic rules or formulas for arriving at this determination. However, the experience of many managers indicates that it takes between three and five years to move from an autocratic to a participative management style. If the management style lies somewhere between the autocratic and participative styles, as most probably do, this time estimate would be shortened.

Management Atmosphere

After concluding its deliberations and decision making with respect to management style and formulating the necessary plans to effect the decisions, management must consider the atmosphere necessary for motivating managers to accept and carry out their share in the participative process. The following paragraphs highlight the minimal requirements of a management atmosphere that motivates rather than controls the actions of subordinate managers. The choice between a good or bad atmosphere clearly is up to management at all levels, particularly at the upper levels.

69

Change and Sacred Cows

Managers should be permitted and encouraged to make hamburger out of sacred cows. Progress usually requires change. Unrealistic custom, practice, policies, and mandates constitute sacred cows. If they preclude or forestall change, they can be a costly impediment to the manager's motivation and contribution. The best management atmosphere encourages managers to make changes in any area or on any subject, if they will lead to improvements. One food company requires as part of its official corporate policy that all major policies and programs which have been in existence for two years be examined in light of the need for changing them. Major breakthroughs and progress made by business have always resulted from change. Wise managers will remember this.

Making Mistakes

The possibility of making mistakes will increase as managers endeavor to make progress through change. Similarly, the magnitude of potential mistakes on the part of high achievers probably increases with the degree to which they aim for meaningful contributions for their units.

Managers who concentrate on day-to-day matters that largely perpetuate the status quo do not expose themselves to many mistakes, and any mistake that might be made is of relatively minor magnitude. Unfortunately, although they may have a low mistake-magnitude record, they often don't accomplish anything significant either.

Management must recognize that the high achiever will endeavor to accomplish more. He will fall on his face from time to time. His record must be reviewed on the basis of what was attempted against what was accomplished. The entire organization will suffer when the manager who hasn't contributed very much but has made few mistakes is given currency over the manager who has contributed but has made mistakes along the line.

Planning the Operation

Each manager should plan for his own operation, and the management atmosphere should recognize and foster this approach. Further, it should emphasize that the manager in charge bears a prime responsibility for determining the destiny of his department.

Proper management atmosphere views profit planning as a joint venture of top management and every source of capability at all levels throughout the organization. In addition to generating positive, profit-making ideas, this participation helps foster general support for profit improvement throughout. The understanding generated by full participation is of particular value. To keep from having top management labeled ruthless or dollar-worshippers, all managers should be familiar with the why and how of profit planning. The understanding that can be gained by wide participation will do much to turn gripers into enthusiastic supporters of the profit-seeking effort.

Feedback

One of the distinguishing features of an achievement-oriented manager is his interest in and demand for feedback on his progress and results. Conversely, the manager who is not achievement oriented cares considerably less about how he is doing and why. Therefore, one of the prerequisites to delegation that brings results is the need to provide each manager with adequate data and information on how well he is carrying out his accountability. Feedback is covered in more detail in Chapters 11 and 12.

Right to Be Heard

As noted in other chapters, much of the success of delegation depends upon the degree to which the subordinate is motivated and committed to carry out his accountability. This commitment is achieved when the manager's thinking

71

reaches the stage in which he regards the success of the delegated assignment as resting entirely on his own shoulders. While he should realize that he may turn to others on occasion for assistance, he must regard himself as being the prime mover for securing the desired results. He must possess a high degree of interest in achieving the results for which he has been delegated the accountability.

For example, a plant manager must regard all operations in the plant as being matters for which he is accountable personally. Any actions affecting operations that are taken by persons who are not located in the plant and do not report to the plant manager will cause him to question his control over the plant's operations. Both his motivation and his commitment suffer when he is given reason to question his control. Thus, to promote the highest possible motivation, the plant manager must be given full opportunity to be heard on any matter that affects the plant before any change is made; the same principle applies to all other managers.

If an order arrives from corporate headquarters to change the plant's production schedule or the area to which it distributes its finished product, and the plant manager is not permitted to address himself to these issues before the changes are made, he will feel that he is no longer accountable for the production and distribution functions. He will be carrying out orders, not managing. As these types of orders increase in frequency, he will begin to think less like a manager. The plant manager must be heard in advance not only on major matters such as production runs and distribution patterns, but on each and every action in the plant—the number of holidays, local work practices, selection of personnel, working conditions, and so on.

Four-Level Delegation

Contrary to popular thinking, delegation involves four levels of management and not just the superior and his subordinate. For ease of reference, refer to the typical organization of a manufacturing operation shown in Figure 5-2. Now consider a delegation between the plant manager and the superintendent in light of the impact the other two levels, the vice president and the foreman, will have on the delegation. First, any delegation the plant manager makes to the superintendent will be influenced heavily by the delegation B has received from A, because B can delegate only within his own accountability. Second, the extent of B's delegation to C and the manner in which he delegates and controls the delegation will be influenced by the manner in which A delegated to B and the control A exerts over the top level delegation.

Assume, for example, that A is the type of manager who requires his subordinates, including B, to have detailed knowledge of his operations at all times and will not permit B to answer "I don't know. I'll have to check with C, who runs that operation." Under these circumstances and similar ones, B is not likely to delegate effectively to C and is likely to overcontrol whatever delegation he does make to C. The

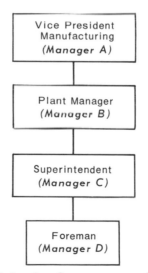

Figure 5-2. Typical levels of management in a manufacturing operation.

entire delegation, down to the lowest level of management, will be influenced by the original delegation from the top.

Similarly, the delegation from B to C will be influenced by D, who reports to C. In the final analysis managers like D carry out much of the accountability B delegates to C. Right or wrong, and it is more wrong than right, B will consider all the management manpower C has available before he (B) delegates to C. The type, extent, and control of the delegation from B will depend considerably upon whether C has an abundance of competent, aggressive people who will accept and carry out delegated accountabilities or a group of average or below par managers who cannot or will not carry out their delegations.

Thus, to achieve its maximum effectiveness in an organization, delegation should be practiced at all levels, and in a consistent and productive manner. Any weakness or failure to delegate at any level will have a decidedly unfavorable impact on the level above and below the one at which the weakness or failure occurs. Once again, such a weakness provides dramatic proof of the old saying that a chain is only as strong as its weakest link. An organizational chain is no exception.

Recognition and Rewards

An organizational atmosphere that promotes and encourages effective delegation must include provision for meaningful recognition to those managers who accept and carry out their accountability. Accomplishment and rewards should constitute a quid pro quo; delegation will be hampered when they don't.

An organization fails when it requires managers to assume extensive accountabilities and complete them in commendable fashion but does not provide meaningful rewards upon accomplishment. Recognition can take many forms—salary increases, incentive compensation, stock options, promotions, and perquisites, among others. There is considerable flexibility in the form of recognition. The key is to provide the recognition *in proportion* to the accomplishment. Major accomplishment should reap major rewards and minor accomplishment, minor recognition.

Recognition through salary and incentive payments provides an excellent example. Many critics of compensation have argued, often strongly, that it is no longer possible to motivate managers through compensation. They attempt to fortify their premise with expressions like "man does not live by bread alone" and say that taxes will take most of the compensation anyway, so why should a manager work harder? These arguments tell only a small part of the story. Certainly if a manager were forced to work 18 hours a day in the middle of the Sahara Desert under a mean, domineering boss, with no vacations and no family or social life, and had to live in a hovel with an outside latrine, it is doubtful that he could be motivated by money. But few managers would work under these circumstances anyway, so the importance of compensation in such a case becomes rather academic.

The primary weakness with most compensation plans and other forms of reward is that they have not been meaningful. A compensation plan that doles out almost equal payments to all managers without regard to the strengths of their accomplishments will not motivate managers to increase or improve the amount of accountability they assume. When manager A achieves results worth ten times the results achieved by manager B, the former should receive ten times the reward received by the latter. All forms of rewards provided by the organization should be tied as closely as possible to accomplishment. The traditional system of giving managers relatively equal rewards in spite of wide differences in the levels of their contributions is unfair and unwise.

Encouragement of Achievement

Dr. Clayton Lafferty, president of Human Synergistics, Inc., and a consulting behavioral scientist to many corpora-

tions, summarizes the major distinctions between an achievement-oriented organization and a nonachievement-oriented
one:

ACHIEVEMENT-ORIENTED	NONACHIEVEMENT-ORIENTED
Emphasize Task Completion	*Increase "Fear of Failure"*
A company-wide commitment to a humanistic emphasis on task completion accompanied by an emphasis on what went wrong, not who. Responsibility is determined, but correction and prevention are emphasized. The employee can then focus on the task, not on defending himself.	Fear of failure produces defensive behavior on the employee's part. Reprimands tend to be toward the person, not the events. Blame is fixed and the person is supposed to feel guilty about the problem. The employee will then defend himself and seldom focus on getting results.
Strengthen Belief in Self-Improvement	*Convince Employee He "Can't Fight City Hall"*
A strong belief at almost every level that the individual by his effort can bring about improvement in the company and in his life. "I can, by my effort, change things." Executives and managers listen. They tend to encourage rather than be threatened by ideas. A good illustration is mentioned by Peter Drucker: A good salesman probably should be able to make more money than the boss.	A strong tendency to bureaucratic control. Information does not move up the pyramid—it always moves down. A tendency to run it by the book, the system, leads to a belief that you can't fight city hall. Luck, fate, chance, and who likes you become the nature of the game. Authority is never mistaken and most problems are handled in a legalistic fashion. The rules prevail. Ideas are not listened to or accepted.
Encourage Cooperative Goal Setting	*Be Arbitrary When You Set Goals*
Goal setting and quota setting activities should be cooperative, take into account the expectations and estimates of the department or person involved. Realistic estimates and facts are the guidelines. There is follow-up and feedback by persons carrying out assignments. It's an ex-	Goal setting and quotas are arbitrary (10% gain this year, men, across the board). Pep talks prevail. No matter how good a performance is turned in, it isn't good enough. Get tough, threaten, do not ask those involved what they estimate— tell them. This is bound to cause

76

ACHIEVEMENT- ORIENTED	NONACHIEVEMENT- ORIENTED

cellent opportunity to listen and see how a man thinks.

people to defend themselves, "look good," try to please you—none of which relate to the task to be accomplished.

Emphasize Hope of Success

Constant attention to the idea that most people are fearful of failure is not exploited, but rather, everything is done to reduce fear of failure and to build management structures that emphasize hope of success at all levels.

Exaggerate Fear of Failure

Common fear of failure is exaggerated by an atmosphere of high anxiety and uncertainty. Performance records are public and the hope is that slow workers will be embarrassed by poor records and improve. It is a common myth about employee behavior that performance is improved by fear.

Engage in One-Way Communications

Allow Full Discussion of Ideas

Appropriate use of conference and discussion techniques designed to get at ideas and attitudes before critical decisions are made. Open questioning of plans and approaches is welcomed. Make it clear that it is the thoughts questioned, not the man.

Little or no use of conference and discussion techniques. Communication is one-way. A company climate where it is commonly perceived as dangerous to disagree. No system of information to top management about feelings and attitudes. If a plan is no good it's implied it's the man who is no good.

Recognize Achievement

Misinterpret Achievement

Real achievement is recognized. Evidence and facts tend to be the ground rules. Ideas are seen against an overall plan of action. Short-term solutions are examined, but always with an eye to the future implications and rewards. Decisions are not impulsive, nor do they depend upon whose ideas, but on the idea itself. Help a man to be able to recognize his accomplishments.

Illusionary achievement is the game. Depends upon recognition and acceptance by superiors. Who looks good and who is "in" are often more important than the skills or the task. Being liked by everyone is no substitute for real achievement. Example: Murray has shown that supermarket managers who were well known to customers tended to be poorer managers. They didn't train the employee to do it, but handled it themselves.

77

ACHIEVEMENT-ORIENTED	NONACHIEVEMENT-ORIENTED
	Put Out the Fires (All the Time?)
Look to the Future	
A management climate that tends to provoke thought about future direction of a department or division or entire company will tend to appeal very much to achievement-oriented persons. It also tends to set a better climate for those more prone to day-to-day crises of management.	Just getting through the next assignment with little or no emphasis on long-range plans can develop a very false sense of well-being in an individual and a company. Persons with low needs to achieve seem to focus excessively on immediate and short-range goals.
Let the Individual Review His Performance	**"You Do It and Not Like It"**
Encourage the employee to talk about his performance to you, including successes, problems, plans, hopes, aspirations, and failures. Draw out in a noncritical way what he thinks about, what he has done or failed to do. Then comment on this. Let him have your ideas but relate them to what he has said.	Conduct a performance review once or twice a year. Let it be characterized by you telling him the good and poor aspects of performance. This procedure assumes the man does not know—it is a process you will avoid because the full burden for questioning is on you.
Create Probability of Success	**Play It Safe**
Set the task at a level where a moderate probability of success is likely. Some uncertainty excites the strongest motivation. Create public and open ways of evaluating success at any given task in the organization. In an achievement climate, people tend not to create self-protective relationships, but tend to conform to an objective reality about standards of success.	Set the task too low or too high. Create high levels of uncertainty and you create defensiveness. Employee will tend to create protective alliances with other employees and a conforming atmosphere develops. Keep the measure of success private and nonpublic, and it arouses suspicion and mutual back scratching. Group pressure prevails—liking a person becomes the standard for judgment rather than objective standards of skill and competence.

SOURCE: Clayton Lafferty, "How Can We Develop Greater Achievement?" *The Hillsdale College Leadership Letter,* 1967.

The prerequisites for delegation, especially the management and organizational atmosphere, constitute the foundation on which the delegation process, per se, is built. The delegation process is much like any type of structure; its ultimate soundness depends upon the soundness of the foundation on which it is built. One of the quicker and more effective ways to administer the coup de grace to delegation is to fail to include the prerequisites in the proper balance when building the foundation.

[6]

THE TRUTHS
OF DELEGATION

THE WISDOM of many delegation principles and practices has become so well established that these principles and practices now constitute truths; in other words, they are the rules of the game for effective delegation. Together, they constitute the climate within which delegation takes place, and the extent to which they are present or lacking helps determine how productive the delegation will be. This chapter examines several of the more important of these truths and explores their applications.

Select the Right Man

Perhaps selecting the right man is one of the more important keys to maximizing the benefits of delegation. Delegating to an incompetent who cannot grow and mature constitutes delegating for the sake of delegation rather than for its benefits. Additionally, the existence of an incompetent in the chain of command imposes an absolute block to delegation:

no delegation can be made to him and he, in turn, can't delegate to those below him.

To determine the level of competence of subordinates, they must be delegated to. Until the subordinate has been given definite accountabilities and authorities, he cannot be measured. A controller in a medium-size manufacturing organization received his initial mandate from the president. It specified that he was the controller and should manage the controller's function. In the months that followed, the president became convinced that the controller was a complete misfit and would probably require replacing. The controller spent an inordinate amount of time in the president's office asking detailed questions and requesting numerous interpretations and guidance. He never seemed to provide data and information in the form desired by the president. Both the president and the controller began chafing under a strained relationship. Subsequent review and analysis by an external consultant resulted in the determination that the controller was especially well qualified in his field and that his ineffectiveness did not come from his inadequacy, but from the president's. The controller had never been told what was expected of him or how much leeway he enjoyed; he had not been delegated to. The natural outgrowth of the fuzzy situation was his floundering and continuous questioning in an attempt to secure guidance.

Thus, a major truth of delegation is that the subordinate should be selected carefully, given accountability and authority, and then provided with the opportunity to develop himself to carry out his delegation.

Delegate the Good and Bad

The ends of delegation are not served if only the unpleasant or distasteful tasks are delegated; both the good and bad should be delegated in a balanced manner. Otherwise, at least three key ingredients of delegation—motivation, commitment, and development—are impeded.

81

The boss cannot overcome these impediments by continually giving the subordinate a big buildup about delegation and its virtues and then never assigning the latter anything but "latrine cleaning" tasks.

One director of industrial relations serves as an outstanding illustration of this practice. Whenever a major grievance is filed by the union or an arbitration case threatens, he assigns one or the other of his subordinate managers to a complete investigation of the problem. This usually involves long hours of interviewing personnel, researching the facts and precedent cases, and writing long, detailed reports and recommendations. When the laborious work has been completed, the director enters the picture and takes over completely. The subordinate never has the opportunity to handle even the most routine cases or issues to conclusion and, in fact, is seldom even permitted to attend the hearings. It is not surprising that these subordinate managers have an extremely high rate of turnover. Their jobs involve little more than researching details.

Take Your Time

Laird and Laird have estimated it takes five years to change from underdelegation to adequate delegation.[1] The reasons would appear to be rather obvious, although they aren't always appreciated and understood. As noted earlier, delegation consists of more than cleaning out the in-basket and dumping its contents on somebody. The foundation must be built, the prerequisites must be met, personnel must be trained both in the technical aspects of their jobs and in the delegation process itself, and their performance must be evaluated to determine how much accountability they can handle. All of these requirements take time. The only way to reduce the time required is to shortcut one of the stages, which usually leads to incomplete and ineffective delegation.

[1] D. A. Laird and E. C. Laird, *The Techniques of Delegation* (New York: McGraw-Hill, 1957).

Delegate Gradually

Closely allied, if not intermingled, with the truth that delegation takes time is the advisability of delegating gradually instead of dumping the whole load on the subordinate at one time. Forcing the subordinate to assume too much accountability at one time can thwart the benefits of delegation, especially when the subordinate is new to the job or has never received much delegation in the past.

A new plant manager, recently promoted from superintendent, reported to a manufacturing vice president who believed firmly that all his plant managers should perform at the same level of competence. He was thus forced to compete with three plant managers who had been on the job for several years. The resulting pressures on the new manager finally culminated in his accepting a superintendent's job with a competitor. The situation might have been avoided if the vice president had delegated more gradually, been satisfied with more modest but continuing achievement, and provided more guidance to the new man. Certainly the chances of success would have been enhanced.

Delegate in Advance

One method of delegation is to wait for a problem or issue to develop and delegate its handling at that time. An alternative and preferable way is to delegate in advance as much as possible. The second alternative permits more planning and time for decision making; the first usually results in the decision being made on the spur of the moment with the disadvantages that frequently attend expediency.

For example, it is common, especially in larger organizations, for the top sales executive to handle troubleshooting with important clients who may be located in one of the areas in which a sales division manager is in charge. When a major customer problem occurs, the top executive may handle it himself. He seldom delegates its disposition to the appropriate division sales manager. As the division manager never really knows when he will be called upon, he is not likely to spend as much time planning to avoid or settle the problem as he would if he knew he were going to handle the problem. A certain number of unexpected problems develop even with the best of planning. However, if the number can be minimized, the ones that do develop won't build up into continual panic situations.

Delegate the Whole

When possible, it is preferable to delegate a whole action to one person rather than a piece of the action to several people. This course facilitates control and coordination and minimizes the possibility of confusion and mistakes. For example, an operation involving shipping of finished goods usually includes receipt of the goods at the shipping area, temporary or permanent storage, order selection and packing, and loading of the product into a truck or other vehicle—four major phases. Each phase could be delegated to a different person, and the four people could each report to the plant manager. However, the plant manager would have to make sure that all four operations were coordinated and controlled properly. A better method would be to delegate the accountability for all four operations to a general foreman or superintendent with authority to mesh all the operations into a balanced whole.

Similarly, in an order-processing operation that includes three related work stages, it is usually better to delegate all three stages to the same person. He is then accountable and can control the operation from beginning to end.

Delegate for Specific Results

Unlike responsibility, which attaches to the job, accountability is an extremely personal matter that attaches only to the individual. For example, the responsibility of the manager in charge of industrial engineering is to carry out the job as head of industrial engineering. His accountability is to accomplish the specific objectives approved for him. In other words, his responsibility is the scope of his job; his accountability consists of the results he must achieve within the scope of the job.

Too often the terms are used interchangeably when delegating and delegation suffers. It is one thing to delegate the responsibility for carrying out the purchasing function. It is an entirely different matter to delegate the accountability for specific results within the purchasing function. The former usually results in vague, general delegation in which it is extremely difficult to measure results. The latter is much preferable as it minimizes confusion and wasted effort by making both the delegation and its measurement better understood by the manager and his superior.

Avoid Gaps and Laps

A gap in delegation occurs when a job must be done, but the accountability for it has not been assigned to anyone. A lap takes place when two or more persons have been assigned accountability for the same job or portion of it.

A research department is headed by a director with four managers reporting to him. The total accountability of the department for any period of time belongs to the five persons who comprise the department. The director must assign each departmental objective to one of his managers or reserve it for himself. If he omits assigning accountability for any objective, he has created a gap or void and the department's performance will suffer. If he assigns accountability in such a way that two or more managers think they are accountable for the same task, he has created a lap, or duplication of effort and cost. The effectiveness of delegation has been lessened in both instances.

In an attempt to minimize the loss in effectiveness of these gaps and laps by spotting them at the earliest possible time, many organizations have departed from the traditional practice of reviewing performance on an annual basis and now hold these reviews monthly or quarterly. The more frequent reviews detect these weaknesses earlier and leave more time for corrective action.

Tie to Level

Delegation usually works better when the magnitude and importance of the task closely follow the manager's level in the organization; his rank should be commensurate with the task. A manager should be required to "stretch" once in a while, but the length of the stretch is pertinent. A modest amount of stretch helps the manager develop; too much stretch may have the opposite effect.

The chances for a successful delegation are weakened when, for example, a young and relatively inexperienced assistant to an executive vice president is delegated a major project such as overall cost improvement for the departments. Although the executive vice president can delegate all the required authority to his assistant, his effectiveness in carrying out the project probably will be seriously hampered by his lack of rank and experience. The success of the project would be enhanced if it were delegated to a senior officer. Similarly, it is seldom desirable to delegate to a foreman tasks that normally should be handled by a superintendent or higher level manager.

A task shouldn't be delegated too high in the organization, either. One of the prime requisites of decision making is that the decision should be made at the lowest possible level at which all the knowledge and information exist for making the decision. The same is true for delegation, of which decision making is an integral part. When a company's general counsel is delegated a task that could and should be handled by his assistant, the company has not made good use of priority of efforts and both the general counsel and his assistant have been done a disservice. The former is working below the level of his talents, and the continued development and interest of his assistant have been thwarted.

Consult Before You Delegate

The best delegation doesn't flow only from the superior to the subordinate. It goes both ways. Power-oriented managers have suffered from their failure to appreciate this truth. They believe delegation flows only from the top to the bottom. In marked contrast to the power-oriented manager, one who is more interested in motivating his subordinates allows them to participate extensively in determining what is delegated to them.

A power-oriented manager was accountable for putting a new production line on stream within 18 months. He determined that five key members of his organization should be involved. He called them together and briefed them on the project. Then, in rapid-fire succession, told each manager: What part he would play in the project, the specific results he must achieve and would be held accountable for, and the allowable time schedule and limit for each result.

This plant manager was delegating, but he allowed only minimal participation by his subordinates. His managers undoubtedly proceeded with little of the motivation and commitment they might have had if they had been allowed to participate actively in each of the steps following the briefing by the plant manager. The probability of success of the total project would have increased if he had briefed them on the demands of the total project and then let each of the five managers recommend his part and schedule in the total project.

Transfer Power

Delegation takes place only if the superior's power has been transferred to the subordinate. If A has delegated to B the accountability for a particular result, A must also transfer his power (authority) to B to accomplish the task; B must have the same authority to accomplish the result A had. If B does not enjoy the same amount of power, complete delegation has not taken place. Both A and B must be involved in carrying out the assignment, as neither manager has complete authority over it. The result invariably is confusion over the delegation and a hesitation to act on the part of the subordinate manager.

Leave the Subordinate Alone

Once the delegation has been made, the subordinate must be left to himself, within the minimal controls discussed in Chapter 12, to carry out the delegation. He must be permitted to make most day-to-day decisions, do his own worrying, and exercise his own ingenuity and resourcefulness. He must be free from all but occasional questions, suggestions, and interruptions by his boss.

Delegation can be destroyed if the boss doesn't give his managers this freedom. A dramatic example is furnished by the owner-manager of one of the better and larger restaurants in New England. Theoretically, at least, the owner has three managers reporting to him—one each in charge of the bar, kitchen, and dining room. The owner is a tough taskmaster and attempts to hold each manager strictly accountable for his part of the operation. However, when the bar gets busy and begins to run three or four drinks behind, the owner jumps behind the bar and takes over. When there is a slight delay in meal preparation, he assumes command of the kitchen. If a waiting line begins to form for the dining room, the owner assumes personal command of seating customers and usually succeeds in fouling up seating arrangements and waitress assignments. His restaurant is characterized by some of the best food served anywhere, one of the highest turnover rates in a high-turnover business, and managers who are permitted to handle only routine matters. Big brother is always watching and quick to take over.

Be Selective in What You Delegate

Every organization undoubtedly has certain duties that should not be delegated. The president may have the final word on acquisitions. The general counsel may be the only one permitted to make statements on pending litigation. Hopefully, the list will be a short one, confined to those items for which there is a valid reason for not delegating, at least below a particular level.

However, no manager should attempt to delegate to others the highly personal area of relationships with one's immediate subordinates. This involves, among other tasks, evaluation and development of subordinates, rewarding and disciplining of subordinates, counseling of subordinates, and the whole raft of interpersonal relationships inherent in a one-to-one relationship. Experience has demonstrated that this ticklish, often frustrating, but important role can be filled successfully only by the immediate superior. Third parties are a poor substitute.

Delegation proceeds more smoothly and brings more lasting results when the truths of delegation are observed and translated into practice. Effective delegation begins with selecting the best possible manager for the job and then providing him with the opportunity for training to insure that his competence is equal to the task. Next, he must be given a meaningful and manageable task to carry out. Finally, he must be provided with the necessary tools and support to carry out his accountability. And he must be left alone to test his own mettle as he strives to achieve the required results.

Laird and Laird indicate that effective delegation takes place when

1. Responsibility is shared with the subordinate.
2. Authority is passed along to help him get it done.
3. Decision making is shared with him or left largely to him.
4. He is given freedom for actions he thinks are needed to reach the objective.

[7]

THE ROLE
OF THE DELEGATOR

TRUE DELEGATION is a tough taskmaster and imposes demanding, but eminently worthwhile, requirements on both the delegator and the delegatee. This chapter examines the role of the superior who is primarily responsible for initiating and controlling the delegation. Chapter 8 covers the subordinate's role. Together, their roles constitute the contract discussed earlier.

Overall Role of the Superior

The willingness of the subordinate to accept and carry out his accountability must be matched by the delegator's willingness to:

1. Establish and use broad controls, that is, maintain control without stifling the subordinate. Reluctance to delegate and trust subordinates often can be traced back to deficiencies of planning and control skills in the superior.

2. Let others make mistakes. Continual checking to eliminate all mistakes will make true delegation impossible.

3. Give up authority to make decisions that can be best or properly made by subordinates. The superior contributes most to company objectives when he concentrates his efforts on the crucial aspects of his position and delegates other tasks, even though he might be able to accomplish these tasks better than his subordinates.

4. Give other people's ideas the opportunity to be discussed and tried.

These four points comprise the superior's overall role. When carrying it out, he must observe and practice several ground rules.

Communicate Clearly

First and foremost, the boss must devote the time and effort to make his requirements known to his subordinate. This is the beginning step and includes giving the delegatee the clearest possible picture of the assignment, the results expected, time limits involved, the authority being transferred to the delegatee, and the form and methods of reporting the boss wants.

It is not enough to communicate these requirements only to the subordinate. All other persons in the organization who may be involved in the assignment must be apprised of the delegation. Otherwise, the delegatee is certain to encounter more than the normal amount of reluctance, misunderstanding, and probably ill feelings on the part of others as he attempts to work with them.

Next, the boss must insure that the delegatee receives a continuous flow of pertinent information as the delegation unfolds. Any information the subordinate needs to carry out the delegation must be provided or his performance will be hampered.

Specify Authority

Granting of authority to the subordinate usually becomes a major stumbling block when there is even the slightest reluctance to delegate. Most superiors are willing to hand out assignments to their people, but they are not equally willing to transfer their own authority to subordinates. This is where the stumbling block can become critical. To be effective, there must be an absolute transfer of power within the agreed-upon parameters. If the boss withholds even the smallest degree of authority within the agreed-upon limits, the delegation is going to suffer.

A division sales manager of a fairly successful company in the machine tool industry is held strictly accountable for sales results in his division. Because of the highly competitive nature of this business, he must have wide discretion over price setting and the ability to make quick decisions. He has missed repeated sales because he has not been given authority over price determination, within even a minimal range, and must check with headquarters before giving even estimated price quotations. It seems sheer folly for this sales manager's boss to preach, as he does, that he has delegated to his managers. The fact that it is both possible and feasible to grant the manager a price range within which he could quote is evidenced by the practices of this company's more successful competitors who do grant this authority.

Encourage Subordinate Participation

Study after study has proven that a subordinate's satisfaction with the job he is given and his motivation to perform it well are highly correlated with the degree to which he believes he has an influence in determining what is expected of him. In contrast, the lowest level of satisfaction and motivation occurs when managers are told what to do and how to do it, when they have little opportunity to display their individual abilities and ingenuity.

The boss who strives to improve his delegating ability will give the widest possible latitude to the subordinate to participate in determining the intent and authority of the delegation. The actions of the head of a corporate division operated on a profit-center basis provide dramatic evidence of the difference participation can effect. The parent corporation expected a four-million-dollar-profit contribution from this division during the coming year. Instead of giving this figure to the manager, his boss briefed the manager on the overall plans and objectives of the parent for the coming year and then said to the manager, "Let's discuss how much profit your division can contribute." After the extensive discussions that followed, the division manager urged that his profit target be set at just under $5 million—an increase of almost 25 percent over the figure the boss might have accepted for him. And the figures a year later indicated that the higher level target was exceeded by an additional $75,000.

Review Results, Not Methods

An effective delegator must also be willing to accept differing solutions for achieving results. Seldom if ever will different managers follow the same approach when solving a problem. Probably all of them will approach it differently than the boss would. The important consideration is whether or not the desired result was achieved, not the particular manner in which it was achieved. Attempts by the boss to influence the approach invariably result in overcontrolling and overdirecting. The natural result is underdelegating. In the process the subordinate's opportunity to develop through using his own initiative and ability is seriously lessened. The poor delegator says, "This is what we are going to accomplish and these are the steps by which we are going to proceed." The effective delegator wisely says, "This is the result we have agreed you will accomplish. Give me your best recommendation for reaching the result."

93

Show Trust

After carefully selecting the delegatee and giving him the clearest possible delegation, the delegator must have the guts and trust to leave him alone to carry out the assignment. The guiding rule should be to check the subordinate's performance only at the checkpoints that are established as minimal controls when the delegation is made initially or when it is obvious that the delegatee is getting into serious trouble. Even in the latter instance, delegation is more effective when the type of relationship is established in which the delegatee comes to the superior for advice and counsel.

Excessive checking and reviewing by the superior soon convinces the subordinate that he really isn't responsible for the assignment and that he needn't worry too much about it because his boss will keep him out of trouble. I am convinced that there is a definite "worry hierarchy" among better management groups; that is, that under proper delegation, each manager must have almost exclusive accountability for worrying about the matters for which he is accountable. If he does not worry about them or if someone else worries about them for him, there has been no true delegation and managerial effectiveness suffers.

I am not inferring that the new delegatee shouldn't be given more attention and guidance than an experienced manager. However, he should be left alone more and more as he gains in experience and competence.

Seek Recommendations

It should be a rare instance when the superior permits the subordinate to request advice and counsel without first asking the subordinate for his recommendation. "What do you recommend?" should be a stock question of all delegators.

This forces the subordinate to think through his own problems and come up with a solution, even if it is not the best one. It precludes the subordinate from being able to toss all problems to his boss without giving any thought to their solution. Also, it permits the boss to evaluate the subordinate's thinking and judgment.

The superior who takes the initiative in answering questions for his subordinates is both a poor delegator and a poor developer of his people. In effect, the superior–subordinate roles become reversed and the boss ends up working for the subordinate—worrying for him, doing his thinking for him, and making his decisions.

Delegate Credit, Not Blame

The boss can and must delegate credit but he cannot delegate blame. How he handles the two helps size him up as a manager. Blame can and must be established, but only between the boss and his subordinate. The boss should not publicize the blame to others or attempt to duck the fact that he bears final accountability for the sins of his people.

One of the most ineffective and disliked managers in my experience was never able to handle the credit and blame facets of his job properly. Whenever a job didn't come off as expected, this manager would grasp every opportunity to denounce the lack of abilities of his people publicly and to disassociate himself with any involvement in the failure. However, the Dr. Hyde side of his managerial personality became highly visible when anyone in the department scored a success that became known outside of the department. In these instances, the manager became sickeningly verbose about how he personally had caused the success. Those not familiar with this manager's modus operandi would have concluded that he must be working 24 hours a day—8 to realize the successes and 16 to make up for the inadequacies of his inept subordinates. He failed to realize, even after being removed from his job, that progressive superiors give high marks to a manager who delegates wisely and develops his people to the point where their contributions can be singled out and heralded. The manager who never is able to credit his people publicly receives poor marks because he's looked upon as a glory hog, a nondelegator, or a manager who must be content with surrounding himself with nonperformers.

Give Support

Once the delegation has been made, one of the more important duties of the superior is to support his people. It should be noted at the outset that the support requirement applies only when the subordinate is right. If he is wrong, it is a disservice to support him. The only recourse in these instances is to let him know he is wrong and help him get turned around as quickly as possible, hopefully in a manner that attracts the minimal amount of attention from others and embarrassment to the subordinate.

Not all delegations proceed smoothly. The delegatee will often be the subject of criticism and doubt as he proceeds. Support from his boss becomes all-important on these occasions. If the subordinate's actions show no sign of being wrong and he is proceeding toward the agreed-upon objective, no amount of criticism from others should cause the boss to withhold his support.

An executive had always been dissatisfied with the security force of the plant and especially the laxness of the guards when persons entered or left the plant. He gave the personnel manager authority to terminate the guards and replace them with a professional security agency from the outside. A couple of days after the change was made, one of the new guards didn't recognize the executive when he tried to enter the plant and required him to identify himself. This incident, plus complaints from the local citizenry about the termination of the 28 company guards, caused the executive to order a change back to the old system and to rehire the former guards. The personnel manager carried out the order and changed back to the old practice. Then he resigned to join another company where he believed he would receive more support for his actions. The decision to change to the outside security agency was a sound one from the standpoints of both cost savings and efficiency; however, the executive permitted the comments of others to cause him to withdraw his support.

Be Consistent

The boss should be a consistent delegator, not one who puts on a campaign from time to time. Delegating only sporadically, especially on the same subject matter, probably causes more confusion and disenchantment in the eyes of the subordinate than any other aspect of the relationship between boss and subordinate.

For example, a New York City organization was housed in a building that was not air-conditioned. A practice had built up over the years of letting the office employees go home whenever the temperature-humidity index reached a certain level. Initially, the office manager would make a recommendation to the controller when the former thought the employees should be dismissed for the day. After the first two or three such recommendations, the controller informed the office manager that he should make these decisions himself based on a certain index number. However, the next time the office manager dismissed the employees on his own initiative, he was reprimanded because the controller had a report he wanted to get out that day and wanted several of the employees to work on it. Naturally, the office manager always sought the controller's approval before closing the office on future occasions. Even worse, the office manager started double-checking almost all his actions with the controller because of the uncertainty about how the controller might look upon them. Ultimately, all this double-checking caused the controller to believe that the office manager was incompetent and he replaced him.

Know Your People

A delegator must know his people, both at the time the delegation is made and as it unfolds. The extent and level of

97

complexity of the delegation must be commensurate with the needs of the organization and with the capabilities and qualifications of the delegatee.

First, the delegator must evaluate the needs of the organization and determine the minimum contribution he must require of the subordinate. Requirements are requirements; if the delegatee cannot meet the minimum there seems little recourse except to replace him. Obviously, this can be tempered if the potential delegatee shows promise and additional time and personnel can be expended during the time he needs to gain increased effectiveness.

Next, the delegator must know how much, above the minimum requirement, he can delegate to the subordinate. He should begin delegating on a modest basis if he has had limited opportunity in the past to size up the subordinate's capabilities. Subsequently, the extent of delegation should be based on the demonstrated performance of the subordinate as gauged by a results-oriented appraisal system; this is discussed extensively in a later chapter.

Develop Your People

One of the more significant benefits of delegation is its value as a developer of people. The delegator assumes the prime role in providing the opportunity and atmosphere for the development to take place. He provides or withholds this opportunity by the manner in which he:

1. Delegates meaningful accountability to the subordinate
2. Permits the delegatee to participate in determining his job
3. Leaves him alone to stand on his own two feet
4. Establishes minimal, but effective, controls for monitoring progress
5. Counsels the delegatee as necessary
6. Rewards or disciplines based on results

The manager who fails to appreciate and understand the developmental aspects of delegation will seldom make an effective delegator as he probably won't be able to put into practice much of the rationale of delegation.

The critical questions the delegator must answer are: What should I delegate? To whom should I delegate it? When or how rapidly should I delegate it? When answering these questions, the delegation will be more effective when the boss (1) studies his job in detail, (2) plans the parts he will delegate, (3) establishes a timetable for carrying out his plans, and (4) trains his subordinates to handle their delegated accountability.

The following items are suggested for delegation to subordinates:

Matters that keep repeating themselves

The minor decisions made most frequently

Details that take the biggest chunks of time

Parts of the job the superior is least qualified to handle

Job details the superior most dislikes

Parts of the job that make the superior overspecialized (for those who wish to be generalists)

Parts of the job that make the superior underspecialized (for those who wish to be more of a technician than a generalist)

However, be careful to insure that the subordinate is given meaningful, challenging assignments and doesn't end up as a dumping ground for the unwanted or distasteful tasks of his superior.

[8]

THE ROLE
OF THE DELEGATEE

THERE MUST BE a meeting of the minds between the boss and his subordinate as to what is to be accomplished and what each party's task is before a delegation "contract" can be effective. If the subordinate is to be more than someone who carries out the boss's orders, he must assume an active and definitive part in the delegation.

Basically, delegation is predicated on the subordinate's willingness to (1) accept responsibility for execution of the duties assigned to him; (2) operate within the limits of the authority granted to his position; (3) put forth his best effort on behalf of his superior and the company; and (4) be held strictly accountable for results. As is true with his superior, he, too, must observe several ground rules when carrying out his role.

Take the Initiative

Delegation becomes more effective when the delegatee takes much of the initiative as to how and what is delegated to him, rather than assume a passive role in which he waits for the boss to speak and then acts on what the boss said.

One of the real impediments to the delegatee exercising initiative in determining his own task is the rather common misunderstanding that delegation flows only from an upper level to a lower level. Actually, delegation works best when both parties have a major voice in determining the delegation. The widespread adoption of the management by objectives system of managing has done much to dispel certain of the misunderstanding through its insistence on objectives for all managers and the requirement that managers recommend their own accountability (results).

The delegatee's chances for success will be enhanced considerably if he recognizes that it's his success or failure, not the boss's, that will be determined by the results. Should the boss delegate improperly, regardless of the cause or weakness, it is the delegatee who is hampered. Even though the boss's total effectiveness may suffer, the bulk of the problem will fall on the delegatee's shoulders.

For this reason, it behooves the delegatee to do everything possible to make certain he receives the best possible delegation. It may be great fun to sit back and gripe about what a poor delegator the boss is, but all the griping in the world isn't going to make the delegatee's job easier or more productive. This can only come about by seizing the initiative and working with the boss to correct the weaknesses.

The boss's initiative should consist of assigning the subordinate to his job, putting him in charge of personnel recruiting, or a cost improvement project, or the development of a new marketing area. In other words, he establishes the scope of the job. He should not try to set the accountability (results) within this responsibility unilaterally.

The delegatee should take the initiative for recommending the results (accountability) within the scope or responsibility. This procedure permits the man to make the job rather than having the boss determine it for him. It also permits the delegatee to exert the full range of his capabilities

101

and drive. In effect, the delegatee should "delegate to himself" through determining as much as possible what he is accountable for.

Relate to the Boss

A few other general thoughts are in order for the delegatee who wishes to improve his performance when working with the boss.

Loyalty. The author has yet to witness a happy subordinate who could not or would not be loyal to his boss. Griping about him behind his back and publicly disagreeing with him are sure signs of disloyalty. Subordinates who believe they are justified in such action should look elsewhere; they will continue to be unhappy, and probably poor performers, until the boss finds out about the situation and removes them. And he will find out about the disloyalty.

Disagreements. Subordinates can and should disagree with their boss. Handled properly, disagreement is healthy and can contribute to better performance by both parties. It helps the delegatee from turning into a yes-man or a follower. There is absolutely nothing wrong with reaching an accord with the boss whereby one can seek a private audience with him and raise "unskirted hell" on a man-to-man basis. The important point is that when the hell-raising session has ended, the disagreement should remain a private matter and both the boss and the subordinate should face the world without letting it know about the heated disagreement—regardless of who won or lost the debate. Resolving disagreements in this fashion marks the healthier management groups.

Improving the boss's results. Another way the delegatee can improve his own lot is to work to make the boss look as good as possible. The wisdom of this approach was summarized well by an Air Force major who had just taken over a new squadron. He told his junior officers, "Your job is to work like hell to get me promoted to colonel and my job is to work equally hard to get you promoted to your next ranks." The wisdom of the major's comment should be obvious. The more successful the boss becomes, the more successful his men will become. Few people can succeed in a sick organization; many can prosper in a successful one.

Be Sure the Delegation Is Realistic

Another potential problem the delegatee should try to avoid is accepting an unrealistic delegation. This is a rather common problem with new managers who want to do a good job, please their boss, and continue to advance. Often they are overly optimistic as to what they can accomplish and they end up by accepting unrealistic delegations.

Prior to accepting a delegation, the delegatee must examine it from every viewpoint. Questions he must resolve include those involving the task, the time allowed, and the resources available to him. Is the task too great (or too small) for the target period? Should the target period be lengthened or shortened? Are the required people, money, and physical resources sufficient to assist in carrying out the task? Is the timing the most conducive to success or should it be changed?

If the delegatee is not able to resolve these questions satisfactorily, he should discuss them with his superior prior to accepting the delegation. Once he has accepted the delegation, it is his problem to live with.

Decide on Your Personal Goals

Countless experience has proven that the more successful managers are those whose personal goals and ambitions closely match the goals of the job and the organization. Before taking on any major delegation, the delegatee should examine the requirements of the task and decide whether or not they are compatible with his own goals. Will the task help him reach his long-term goal or is it contrary to it? Is he

103

willing to make the sacrifices that may be required in time, travel, or relocating? Will his boss and the people in the work group be the type he likes to work with? Will the tempo or pace of the job be consistent with his makeup? Does he want to take on the increased responsibility or is he happier as an Indian than as a chief?

Although much has been written and spoken about the problems resulting from trying to place square pegs in round holes, it continues to happen as managers take on additional responsibilities without first reflecting on their personal goals.

Determine Your Feedback

Much to be sympathized with is the manager who permits someone else to determine what feedback he will receive on his operations. He receives information someone else thinks is important, not necessarily what he needs to monitor his operation. Yet many managers continue to receive worthless reports that serve no purpose week after week and month after month.

Chances are that whenever a manager damns the accounting or financial department for creating a useless paper mill the fault is more that of the manager than of accounting. No accounting department, with only minor exceptions, wants to spend hours preparing reports that aren't used. However, in the absence of specific guidance from the manager as to what is important to him and what he needs, accounting personnel must use their own judgment, which is often isolated from operating details and methods.

Useful information can result only from a joint effort by the manager and information assemblers. The input from the manager is a description of the important aspects of his operation and the type and frequency of the information he can use to run his operation better. Accounting's input is to decide the best method of collecting, analyzing, and distributing the information. One management authority has stated that the first thing he would do if he were in charge of a company would be to summarily withhold all financial and accounting reports from managers. He believes many of them would not be missed because they aren't being used.

Every manager has a critical stake in feedback. If he isn't getting the right type, he is missing an opportunity to help him carry out his accountability. In addition, if the manager himself isn't receiving proper feedback, he will have a more difficult task reporting to the boss. Feedback and controls are discussed in detail in Chapter 12.

Report to the Boss

The specific content, detail, and frequency of reporting to the boss will depend on the nature of the delegation and the requirements he establishes. It is of paramount importance in this connection for the delegatee to reach a clear understanding with the boss as to what the reporting requirements are. Should the boss be vague or overly general in his instructions, the delegatee should bore in and endeavor to get specifics. Here again, the burden is on the subordinate to learn what is expected of him.

In general, minimum reporting should include the following:

1. Interim status reports on long-term projects
2. Reports of completed projects and results achieved as against planned results
3. Reasons and action recommended to compensate for the variance when plans do not develop as anticipated
4. Major, unanticipated obstacles or problems, including recommended handling
5. Any confusion in the extent of the delegation or authority needed
6. Recommendations for improving the job, the department, or the organization as a whole

Except when the delegatee is completely stumped—in which case he should openly admit his predicament—all reports to the boss should be accompanied by a recommendation, especially when problems or unfavorable variances are involved. The delegatee must think through his own problems before confronting someone else with them.

Carry Out the Delegation

The first job of the delegatee is to carry out the delegation and achieve the end results. His measure as a manager is based on successful accomplishment. One of the marks of an effective manager is the delegatee's willingness to devote the time and thought to developing concrete, realistic plans for reaching his objectives. He must also be completely unwilling to change the objectives downward when an unexpected circumstance causes an unfavorable variance until he has exhausted all possible alternative courses of action.

A weak manager tries to change his objective every time some problem occurs. A superior doesn't seek subordinates who fall in the latter category; he tries to avoid them or get rid of them. When he delegates he's looking for a manager who will help enhance his own (the delegator's) contributions, and he knows the best subordinate is one who endeavors to solve problems rather than duck them.

Develop Yourself

When he accepts the delegation the delegatee also accepts the responsibility for developing himself in whatever manner the delegation requires or provides. The delegatee must recognize that no one else can develop him, he must do it himself. If the delegation requires him to be more proficient, say, in financial analysis, he must plan the means and execute them to become more proficient. The boss must provide the opportunity but the subordinate must do the performing. This is especially true at the higher levels of an organization, where the manager is assumed to be very competent and little formal attention is paid by others to his training and development. If he has definite weaknesses when he gets to these upper levels, chances are that others won't recognize his need for training until he has failed or is about to.

Completed Staff Action

One of the better summaries of the subordinate's role in delegation is set forth in the following statement of what constitutes completed staff action:

1. *Completed staff action* is the study of a problem—and a presentation of a solution by an employee in such a form that his supervisor or department head may simply indicate approval of the *completed action.*

The words "completed action" are worth real emphasis. Actually the more difficult the problem is, the more tendency there is to present the problem to the supervisor in piecemeal fashion. It is your responsibility as an employee to work out the details. You should *not* consult your supervisor in the determination of these details unless necessary. Instead, if you cannot determine these details by yourself, you should consult other persons.

In far too many problem situations the typical impulse of the inexperienced man is to ask the supervisor what to do. And this recurs more often when the problem is difficult. It is accompanied by a feeling of mental frustration. It seems to be much easier to ask the supervisor what to do. And appears to be so easy for him to give you the answer. You must resist that impulse. You will succumb to it only if you do not know your job.

It is your job to *advise* your supervisor what *he* ought to do—not to ask him what *you* ought to do. He needs answers—not questions! Your job is to study, analyze, check, restudy and recheck until you have come up with a single proposed action—the best one of all that you have considered. Your supervisors may then approve or disapprove. In most instances, completed work results in a single document prepared for the signature of the supervisor, without *accompanying comment.*

Except for record purposes, writing a memorandum *to your supervisor,* therefore, does *not* constitute completed work. Writing a memorandum *for your supervisor to send to someone else does.*

Your views should be placed before him in *finished form* so that

107

he can make them his views simply by signing his name. If the proper result is reached by your "in finished form" solution to a problem, the supervisor will usually recognize it at once. If he needs comment or explanation, he will ask for it.

The requirements for completed work do not put aside the possibilities of a "rough draft" in place of a "highly finished form" in approaching some of the problems. *But* a rough draft must *not* be a half-baked idea! Neither must a rough draft be used as a means for shifting to the supervisor the burden of formulating the action. It must be *complete in every respect* except that it lacks the requisite number of copies and need not be neat.

2. *Completed work* requirements may result in more work for the employee, but provide more freedom for the supervisor. This is as it should be, since it accomplishes two things:

The supervisor is protected from half-baked ideas, voluminous memoranda, and immature oral presentments.

The man who has a real idea to sell is enabled more readily to find a market.

3. *Test the completeness of your work* by asking yourself this question:

If you were supervisor, would you be willing to sign the paper you have prepared, and stake your professional reputation on its being correct?

If the answer is no, take it back and work it over because it is not yet completed work.[1]

Much of what is delegated will be determined by the delegatee himself, subject to concurrence from his boss. The delegatee must assume the lion's share of answering the all-important question of whether or not he is willing and capable of handling the delegation. The boss makes a preliminary determination of the answer when he first considers the delegation. However, in the final analysis, the delegatee must provide the key to the answer. If his answer is in the affirmative, the success of the endeavor will be determined in large part by the amount of initiative he exercises to control his own corporate destiny.

[1] "Completed Staff Action," *Guide to Administrative Action* (Washington, D.C.: U.S. Air Force, 1952).

[9]

WHAT DELEGATION REQUIRES OF THE JOB DESCRIPTION

JOB DESCRIPTIONS have a role of prime importance to serve in the delegation process. However, if they are to serve their vital purpose, several complete departures must be made from the manner in which most descriptions have been prepared in the past.

An effective job description should serve as the basis for:

1. Recording the delegated responsibility and accountability
2. Developing plans for meeting objectives
3. Guiding the incumbent in his day-to-day actions
4. Controlling the delegation as it unfolds
5. Measuring the incumbent's performance
6. Providing concrete evidence for rewarding or disciplining

Thus, the job description should serve as the major instrument for recording the delegation.

The reader is given notice, prior to reading the remainder of this chapter, that it contains what may constitute radical departures from the traditional approach and thinking with respect to job descriptions and their use, and the definition and use of such words as "responsibility" and "accountability." Those sensitive to departing from tradition could easily take considerable exception to this approach. Hopefully, these persons will strive for objectivity as they read this and other chapters in this book.

This approach is not the only one, but it is a practical, dynamic one that has achieved considerable success in many different organizations. It can bring reality to what often has been merely a quagmire of paperwork, forms, words, and filing material.

Common Weaknesses: How to Overcome Them

Chapter 4 summarized and highlighted the major reasons the ordinary job description does not serve its required role in the delegation process. These reasons are:

1. Emphasis is placed on activities to be pursued rather than results to be achieved.

2. Sufficient emphasis is not devoted to revising the description to reflect the changing priorities of the organization. Typically, the same description remains on the books year after year.

3. There is no provision for continual improvement from one period to the next because the descriptions seldom change.

4. Job descriptions, by their very name and nature, emphasize the job rather than the man even though the man makes the job, not vice versa. And the greater the degree of delegation, the more the man makes the job.

It is, of course, entirely possible to compensate for several of these weaknesses by supplementing the traditional job description with other documents and forms. For example, the weakness of an "activity" orientation can be mitigated by a supplemental list of specific objectives the incumbent must achieve over a short-run period. However, supplementing the basic document involves considerable unnecessary time, effort, and cost. Instead, why not include in one dynamic document all key components of the delegation? It is possible as illustrated in the ensuing paragraphs.

Construction of an effective job description for use in delegation constitutes a process of continuously zeroing in on the specific accountability of the incumbent. First, it should outline the broad responsibility of the incumbent (the scope of his job). Next, it should list the key-results areas in which he must perform within the scope. Third, it should specify the objectives he must accomplish within the key-results areas (his accountability). Lastly, the job description sets forth the authority he has been delegated.

For delegation purposes, the job description must be looked upon as being a living, dynamic document that is manager-oriented rather than job-oriented and filed away once it is written, as all too frequently happens with many job descriptions. Figure 9-1 outlines the major sections and content of a dynamic job description and emphasizes the timing factor involved for each section. Later paragraphs of this chapter suggest placing the emphasis where it belongs by changing the title to "Statements of Accountability."

Responsibility Versus Accountability

Many writers and, to a lesser extent, practitioners have done an excellent job of confusing and clouding the difference between responsibility and accountability. It is not the intent of this section to delve deeply into semantics; however, the distinction between these two words is of major significance in the delegation process.

Responsibility describes the manager's global assignment: he's in charge of the financial function or he's the manager

Figure 9-1. Key components of a job description for delegation purposes.

I. *Scope* (Responsibility)

  A. Content

    1. The major functions and/or personnel assigned to him

    2. The parameters of his responsibility

      a. By organizational unit, for example, corporatewide, subsidiary, plant, division, department

      b. By geographical area, for example, United States, Eastern Division, worldwide

  B. Time Factor. This section is changed only when a revision is made in the responsibility; for example, a function or department is added or subtracted.

II. Key-Results Areas

  A. Content. The primary areas (usually six to eight), within his scope, which comprise the true mission of his job—the real reason his job exists. Example: Two of the key areas for a sales manager would be optimizing sales and controlling selling costs.

  B. Time Factor. A manager's key-results areas may change from one target period to the next, but not necessarily, depending on whether the company's priorities have changed.

III. Objectives (Accountability)

  A. Content. The specific results the manager must achieve during the target period.

  B. Time Factor. Objectives almost always change from one target period to the next and often during the target period itself.

IV. Authority

  A. Content. The power that has been transferred to the manager to carry out his objectives.

  B. Time Factor. Must change as often as necessary to remain consistent and compatible with any changes in responsibility and objectives.

---

of finance; he's in charge of personnel or the personnel manager. Responsibility establishes the fences around the operating area the manager directs. It can be viewed as an arena in which he conducts his managerial actions. It is more general than accountability in that it does not spell out the specific results to be achieved.

For example, the responsibility of a typical financial officer might include directing the following functions: capital management, accounting, data processing, office services, and reporting systems. These constitute his operating area. They do not include the results he must achieve in these five major functions.

Accountability, on the other hand, is quite specific and details the concrete results the manager must produce. It flows logically from responsibility. In the preceding example the financial officer was in charge of capital management—a responsibility. Next, the financial manager is asked, "What concrete objectives are you going to achieve within your responsibility for capital management?" His answer, expressed in the form of objectives, constitutes his accountability.

Table 9-1 sets forth the major differences between responsibility and accountability. It shows that responsibility is more job related and a higher degree of it is assigned to the manager by his superior. When a manager is promoted or otherwise placed in the job of a purchasing manager, much of his responsibility has been assigned to him. If he accepts the job he has agreed to take over the jurisdiction within the fences or boundaries of the purchasing manager's job. Of course, he can recommend modifications to the job's responsibility. To the extent his recommenations are approved he has influenced his responsibility. However, the bulk of his responsibility was assigned to him when he agreed to accept the job. This should cause no great concern to him, provided he is given the opportunity to participate in determining what he will make of the job.

This decidedly is not true with accountability if both the superior and the subordinate are knowledgeable about ef-

Table 9-1. Comparison of responsibility and accountability.

RESPONSIBILITY	ACCOUNTABILITY
General	
Indicates the scope of the manager's job or the major functions he directs; for example, he is a personnel manager or a purchasing director	States the results he must achieve within his responsibility; for example, sell 100 units at a per-unit price of $2,000, or effect a cost improvement of $10,000
Specific	
Is usually assigned, manager has less opportunity to influence	Is delegated, manager has wide latitude to influence
Used to build organization charts	Key to delegation
Job related (more impersonal)	Manager related (highly personal)
General (says where he works)	Specific (tells what he must accomplish)
Only loose control possible	Tight control possible
Ongoing, seldom changes	Self-liquidating, should change at end of each target period
Specific authorities not established	Specific authorities must be established
Performance measurement almost impossible	Performance measurement possible and highly desirable
Poor basis for compensation beyond base salary	Most equitable basis for compensation beyond base salary
Management development is general	Management development is specific
Poor motivator (what should I be doing, how much authority do I have?)	Effective motivator (I know what I should do and how much authority I have)
Usually expressed in a traditional job description (as activities to pursue)	Better expressed as objectives (to be achieved)

fective delegation and are practicing it. The superior should ask, "What are you going to do within your responsibility (what are your objectives?)?" He should be giving the subordinate the widest possible latitude to recommend his own accountability. Current evidence suggests that managers who have the most opportunity to determine their own accountability will accept it with much more commitment and carry it out with greater motivation than managers whose accountability is assigned to them. Therefore, while it is descriptive to refer to the job or responsibility as being assigned, accountability should not be assigned. The subordinate should be given maximum opportunity to participate in determining it. It then becomes largely his own creation rather than a list of chores foisted upon him by his boss.

Statement of Accountability

One way to minimize the impact of the weaknesses of the traditional type of job description is to call it a "statement of accountability" instead. Although labels normally are not too important, a twofold benefit would result through this substitution. First, the latter label emphasizes the personal nature of accountability; it goes with the manager and not with the job. The manager gets results, not the job. Second, it emphasizes that the manager makes the job, not vice versa. The usual job description describes the job in the same terms for all managers assigned to that job. A statement of accountability, on the other hand, enumerates the results or objectives desired in terms of the individual.

Three managers may be assigned the responsibility inherent in the job of assistant general counsel. However, there probably will be wide differences among the objectives for which each incumbent will be accountable. The differences in objectives will reflect differences in the company's requirements and in the experience, capability, drive, and initiative of each manager. Thus, in marked contrast to

115

job descriptions, the actual content and demands upon the incumbents will vary greatly when statements of accountability are used—even when job titles are the same.

Figures 9-2 and 9-3 illustrate the construction of statements of accountability for a vice president of finance and a director of marketing, respectively. Each has been constructed using the format that progresses from scope to key results to objectives. The "authority" portion of the statement of accountability is discussed in Chapter 11.

Key-Results Areas

It is not absolutely essential for key-results areas to be included in a statement of accountability, but their inclusion can help the manager insure that he is translating his responsibility into high-priority objectives. They are a natural intermediate step in moving from responsibility to accountability.

Key-results areas may be defined as the primary aspects of the manager's job—his true mission. They guide the manager toward setting his priorities in terms of time and effort in a manner designed to realize the greatest return. They give real meaning to Dr. Drucker's counsel, quoted in Chapter 1, that "managers must allocate resources, especially high-grade human resources, in the manner which provides opportunities for high economic results."

Key-results areas should always be delineated before the manger writes his objectives; the latter should flow from the former. Table 9-2 demonstrates the undesirable consequences of writing objectives before selecting the key-results areas. All three managers involved in Table 9-2 moved too quickly to the writing of objectives without first selecting the key-results areas of their jobs. As a consequence, the bulk of their objectives concerned rather routine, low-priority matters. Figures 9-2 and 9-3 illustrate key-results areas for the jobs described.

Figure 9-2. Abbreviated statement of accountability for a vice president of finance.

RESPONSIBILITY

As the senior financial officer of the company he reports to the president and is responsible for directing the following functions on a corporatewide basis: capital and operating budgets, capital management, credit and collection, data processing, accounting systems and practices, internal auditing, and financial analysis.

The following report to him: controller, treasurer, budget director, data processing manager, manager of financial analysis, manager of credit and collections, and manager of internal auditing.

KEY-RESULTS AREAS

1. Accurate and timely measurement of operations
2. Reporting of data for decision making
3. Costs of purchases of office equipment, supplies, and materials
4. Investment of funds
5. Security of corporate assets
6. Capital availability and cost

ACCOUNTABILITY—1974 (OBJECTIVES)

1. Establish necessary lines of credit to insure minimum borrowing power of $20 million is available by September 1 at a rate not to exceed 1 percent over prime for use in making approved acquisitions.
2. Achieve a minimum profit improvement (over 1973) of 1 percent on short-term investments (less than six months) and 0.5 percent on long-term investments (six months to two years) based on the average funds available for investing on the first day of each month.
3. By July 1, submit a "make or buy" recommendation on the company's data processing division detailing justification for continuing division within company versus going to an outside service bureau. Recommendation to hinge on:
   (a) Comparison of costs to company
   (b) Speed and quality of output
   (c) Probable requirements for next ten years
   (d) Reliability
4. Reduce from ten to seven days following the last day of each month the distribution of the monthly report of operations.

Figure 9-3. Abbreviated statement of accountability for a director of marketing.

RESPONSIBILITY

Reports to the president and directs, companywide, the development and execution of sales objectives, programs, and policies, including those for product sales, advertising and promotion, market and consumer research, sales training, and customer relations.

Reporting to him are the general sales manager, director of advertising, director of market research, manager of sales training, and manager of customer relations.

KEY-RESULTS AREAS

1. Sales forecasting and planning
2. Gross margin of sales
3. Selling expense
4. Distribution channels
5. Sales manpower development
6. New market development

ACCOUNTABILITY—1974 (OBJECTIVES)

1. Achieve total sales volume and gross margin on sales within plus or minus 5 percent of budget.
2. Reduce private-label sales by 15 percent from 1973 levels without loss in total sales volume.
3. Train minimum of ten assistant regional sales managers to level of competence capable of performing as regional sales managers by August 1.
4. Develop new Detroit regional market so that a 28 percent market-share position is achieved by July 1 at total development costs of $75,000, with total introduction and promotion costs not to exceed 10 percent of average retail selling price of the other 19 divisions.
5. Complete market and consumer tests of new product X by March 1 and submit go or no-go recommendation by April 15.

Table 9-2. Results of failure to select key-results areas first.

	JOB VIEWED AS	LOW-PRIORITY OBJECTIVES
Controller	1. Maintain accounting records	1. Reduce cost of accounting records by 5%
	2. Prepare reports	2. Submit monthly operations report by fifth day of month
	3. Administer budget program	3. Investigate and report on all variances exceeding plus or minus 5%
Purchasing	1. Process purchase orders and requisitions	1. Process all requisitions within 3 days of receipt
	2. Place orders	2. Place all orders within 5 days
	3. Assure deliveries	3. Maintain on-time delivery schedule
Public Relations	1. Secure news releases	1. Place 3 articles per month
	2. Write speeches for executives	2. Write all speeches one month in advance
	3. Promote community relations	3. Arrange annual open house

Practical Differences

The difference between operating under the ordinary job description and a comprehensive statement of accountability is illustrated by the experiences of the vice president of research of a manufacturing company with sales approximating $25 million. The average research budget for the past five years had been about $1 million, or 4 percent of sales, an unusually high ratio for companies in this industry.

119

His job description spelled out his delegation in highly relative terms:

1. Responsible for and has commensurate authority to accomplish the duties delegated to him.

2. Develops and recommends such corporation-wide technical research policies and programs as are necessary to support profitable growth and implement the general policies and goals of the corporation.

3. Coordinates such research activities as the operating divisions may undertake and advises the president of any unnecessary duplication.

4. Stimulates and encourages the operating divisions in increasing the adequacy and quality of their research programs.

5. Establishes and administers the company's central research laboratory, whose functions are: (a) Investigate new ideas which, if successful, can provide the operating divisions with the basis for future products or processes. (b) Within the discretion of the director of research, assist the operating divisions on technical problems which arise during the course of their work, especially if the problem is common to more than one division.

The actual job description contained 14 separate duties. For brevity, only five representative ones are included here. But it can be seen that the general nature of this job description provided little guidance to the research director as to what he should accomplish. This undesirable condition was compounded further by the lack of any overall corporate objectives to assist him. About the only guidance available to him was an occasional request from an operating division for some research work. Little guidance was received from the president, who had come up through the ranks and had little understanding of research matters.

During the five years under consideration, the research director's natural bent for basic or pure research took over. This period was characterized by an average of 45 major research projects at any one time. Only a few of them bore any relationship to the company's primary businesses. Exotic research projects followed one upon the other. The return on research expenditures was worse than minimal and the entire department suffered a very low degree of acceptance within the company. Competent research personnel stayed for only short periods of time; the less competent stayed forever.

A temporary slump in the company's fortunes culminated in a complete reexamination of the research effort. With the assistance of a management consultant, a statement of accountability was drawn up indicating the specific accountabilities research was delegated. A similar statement was developed for each of the top managers within the research division. The reorientation of the research function caused its director to resign. He was replaced by a results-oriented manager, and within two years, dramatic changes began occurring in research effectiveness. Each man knew what he must accomplish; this alone brought a new sense of purpose to the division. Total research expenditures decreased by almost 30 percent while the return on research expenditures increased by an estimated 60 percent. Total research efforts became closely allied with the company's real needs. Internal acceptance of the research function has now reached the point where it is considered a valuable part of the company's operation.

Standards of Performance

Certain organizations endeavor to spell out accountability in more detail than that provided for by the manager's objectives. First, the manager recommends his objectives, which are addressed to the highest priorities of his job during the target period; the more routine parts of his job are not covered by objectives. Several organizations require these more routine aspects to be covered by what is frequently called "standards of performance." For example, it may be company policy that a purchasing director place all orders within three days after receiving a purchase requisition. This would become a standard of performance, not an objective, for him. An accounting manager's standard of performance might be to distribute a certain accounting report within five days after the close of an accounting period. Making an input to the computer within five days of receiving the necessary data is an example for a data processing manager. Having at least 90 percent of the employees report to work on time might be a standard for an office manager.

Extreme care must be exercised when utilizing standards of performance to insure that violence is not done to effective delegation through overcontrol and interference with the means or methods by which the manager accomplishes his overall job. After all, the end result should be spelled out in his accountability, not the means by which he reaches it.

Experience would seem to argue against the extensive use of detailed standards of performance. The more routine parts of the job should not be covered by either objectives or standards of performance. However, should a routine task be neglected or handled so poorly that it becomes a major problem, its priority can be changed to justify including it as a major objective. After the problem is solved, it would return to the routine category. This practice is followed by many organizations and is more compatible with the principles of delegation.

A written document is required to aid in clarifying and embodying the delegation to both the delegator and the delegatee when the delegation is made and later. Otherwise, there is the chance of confusion and misunderstanding as the delegation proceeds. Historically, attempts have been made to have the job description serve this purpose. It may have served with some success as a guide for evaluating jobs for rate-setting and selection and training purposes, but its rather static and impersonal characteristics render it wholly inadequate as the primary instrument for hard-hitting delegation. Statements of accountability overcome the weaknesses of job descriptions and, as living, viable documents they facilitate the delegation process. As a side effect, switching from job descriptions to statements of accountability usually results in less paperwork, and less work and costs for typists, file clerks, and job analysts. A more comprehensive, harder-hitting aid to delegation is realized at less cost.

[10]

DELEGATION
BY LEVELS

ONE OF THE more thought-provoking problems in delegation is to determine which matters should be delegated and which should be retained. And, if the acccountability should be delegated, to which level? Although there are no magic rules for arriving at the distinction, the superior should begin his analysis by observing five general guides:

1. Matters that can be handled adequately down the line should be delegated.
2. If all the information necessary for decision making is available down the line, consideration should be given to delegating the matter.
3. The more the matter involves operational detail, as contrasted to planning and organization, the more the matter should be considered for delegation.
4. Matters unique to the superior or his job should not be delegated.
5. Matters over which others have direct control usually should be delegated.

Delegate More at Higher Levels

Organization charts are drawn to resemble a pyramid with the apex at the top. Unfortunately, such pictorial representations do not reflect one of the more important principles underlying delegation; namely, the higher up one moves in an organization the more opportunity he has to influence the job and the more opportunity he has to determine the extent and type of delegation that takes place.

Figure 10-1 is an organization chart based on the ability of particular levels of management to influence the job and the necessity for delegation. As one moves up the management ladder he becomes less and less involved in operational details and more and more responsible for planning, organizing, and controlling. Consider the extreme ends of the management hierarchy. At the very top we have the president, who should devote almost his entire attention to planning and little, if any, to operational detail. On the other hand, the foreman at the bottom may spend 80 percent of his time intimately involved in the operational detail; this detail is the fallout resulting from the planning done by the president and managers at intermediate levels.

The higher the manager is in the hierarchy the more op-

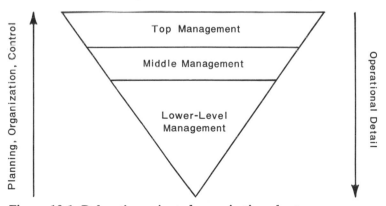

Figure 10-1. Delegation-oriented organization chart.

125

portunity he has to delegate and the more he must delegate. Conversely, the lower the manager is on the ladder the less his opportunity and requirement to delegate are. This doesn't mean he shouldn't delegate, but that his scope for delegating is more limited than at higher levels.

There are two principles at work here:

1. The higher up he is in the organization, the more opportunity the manager has to influence the job and his accountability.
2. The percentage of time spent on planning, organization, and control increases up the line. Operational detail increases down the line.

The difference in the scope of opportunity for delegation has two causes. First, the higher the manager proceeds up the organization chart the more he makes the job. At lower levels, the job has more of an impact on the man in it. For example, the president has almost unlimited opportunity to structure his own job, while much of a foreman's job is determined by the work requirements of his operation and the objectives and policies that have been set at higher levels. The typical president probably delegates 85 to 90 percent of his job, but a foreman can delegate about 25 percent of his.

Second, at the higher levels, managers must divorce themselves from operating details so that they may devote the majority of their time to planning, organizing, and controlling. These three functions become increasingly overshadowed at the lower levels by the responsibility for supervising, meeting schedules, and paying attention to details. A foreman's accountability tends to be influenced heavily by such constraints as corporate and departmental objectives, collective bargaining agreements (especially work rules), and the fact that there are no lower level managers over whom he has control and to whom he can delegate.

Laird and Laird have suggested the following arbitrary, but useful, percentages of how much should be delegated at various management levels: president, 95; vice president, 75; department head, 50; and foreman, 25.[1]

R. Alec MacKenzie quotes Ralph C. Davis, who provides a further breakdown by distinguishing between "managing" (supervising subordinates) and "operating" (doing things yourself). MacKenzie suggests the following: [2]

Level	Managing	Operating
Chief executive	90%	10%
Vice president	70	30
Middle management	50	50
First-line supervisor	30	70

This distinction between managing and operating again underscores the difference between insuring something is done—managing subordinates—and doing it yourself—being involved in operating details.

Naturally, these estimates of the extent to which delegation should take place at various levels do not mean that once the manager has delegated he is left with a part-time job; for example, that a president who delegates 90 percent is left with only 10 percent of a job. The manager must simply reallocate the time he spends. As he delegates more and more of the operational detail, the time he formerly spent on operations is now devoted to planning, organizing, and controlling. He now becomes more heavily involved in determining priorities, planning based on the priorities, and insuring that necessary action is taken by others. In short, he sees that action is taken rather than acting himself.

For example, the bulk of operational detail for a sales department usually consists of the actual merchandising, selling, and servicing of the account. Prior to examining his delegation practices, a vice president of sales had been spending approximately 35 percent of his time handling many aspects of this operational detail. After delegating it

[1] D. A. Laird and E. C. Laird, *The Techniques of Delegation* (New York: McGraw-Hill, 1957), p. 52.
[2] R. Alec MacKenzie, *The Time Trap* (AMA, 1973), p. 130.

127

down the line where it belonged, he was able to devote much of the 35 percent to tasks that more properly belonged at his level—sales policy determination, sales strategy, market research, and supervision of his subordinates.

Delegate Based on Uniqueness

Before delegating, the superior should decide what his unique contribution should be within his total accountability. This helps him to avoid delegating merely a smaller version of his own job. For example, a sales vice president usually is accountable for sales revenues, sales expense, sales training, distribution areas and channels, product line, and trade relations. Of these six major accountabilities, at least three of them—sales revenues, sales expense, and sales training—come from, and are primarily controlled by, the line sales managers who report to the vice president, not the sales vice president himself. The sales vice president's unique contributions are in the broader areas of determining distribution areas and channels and products to be sold, and handling trade relations. He should delegate the first three and retain the latter three as matters in which he can make a unique contribution.

The undesirable alternatives are:

1. Retain a piece of all six duties and delegate a piece of all six to each sales manager. The superior and his managers will be in each other's hair continually as to who is supposed to do what.

2. Delegate all six duties to the sales managers. The superior will become little more than a bookkeeper keeping records of what his managers accomplish. Although over-delegation is rare, this is the way it usually happens.

Select Key-Results Areas

One of the best methods for determining to which level a function should be delegated is to begin by selecting key-results areas. These can be defined as the end result that must be achieved by any activity undertaken. They constitute the real purpose of the job—the justification for the existence of the job.

For example, a financial manager is not employed to keep books. He merely uses these tools of his trade to accomplish something else. A purchasing manager is not paid to process purchasing requisitions and orders; these, too, are merely tools or means to an end.

Key-results areas are concerned with ends, not means. One of the ends of a financial manager's job is the timely and accurate measuring of organizational performance. To accomplish this end, he maintains books and records (the means).

Key-results areas concentrate on the "what," not the "how." The "what" in the financial manager's job consists of the accurate and timely measurement. The books and records comprise the "how."

Finally, key-results areas concentrate on the ultimate output rather than the efforts expended to reach the output. Typical key-results areas for a financial manager are:

1. Accurate and timely measurement of operations
2. Data and recommendations for decision making
3. Cost savings (for own department's accountability, such as purchases of office equipment, supplies, materials)
4. Cost of capital
5. Capital inflow
6. Capital availability
7. Return on investable funds
8. Optimum cost of departmental operations
9. Security of corporate assets

Key-results areas should be decided upon before determining at what level of management they should be accomplished and delegated. These areas serve as a guide to the appropriate level. The manager at the level of management to which the key result is delegated can then tailor his accountability by recommending his objectives and the authority he will require to carry them out. The prior selection of key-results areas helps avoid having objectives written at the wrong level and by the wrong manager. Often, it avoids having the objective passed down the line to a manager who had little voice in developing it.

Key-results areas also help avoid overlooking certain critical aspects that must be covered by objectives. If a manager starts structuring his objectives without giving adequate attention to the key-results areas, he will lack the guidance they provide as to the total content of his accountability. He may develop six or eight meaningful objectives but they may not cover his total accountability in a particular area.

For example, as we shall see later, a plant manager usually has as one of his key-results areas the accountability for attaining a stipulated return on the assets entrusted to him. This return is calculated on the basis of both present assets and capital expenditures that may be approved in the future. Unless he first determines his key-results area as being return on assets his objectives might cover only the return on present assets.

Key-results areas are like an umbrella. First we determine who should have the umbrella. Then we determine the number and type of spokes (objectives) required to support the umbrella properly. We will now illustrate the use of key-results areas for determining and tailoring ultimate accountability.

Store Operations

The store operations department of a large, Midwestern grocery distribution and sales company was organized as illustrated in Figure 10-2. A major question arose in the company when efforts were made to establish the key-results areas for the regional manager to whom the individual store managers (profit center heads) reported. The president, during an in-depth discussion with all senior executives, offered the strong opinion that the regional manager could be

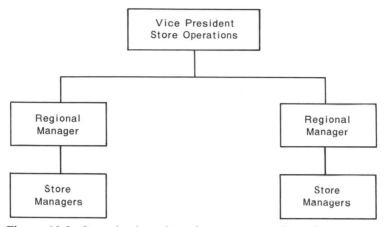

Figure 10-2. Organization chart for store operations department of a grocery sales company.

held accountable only for the sum of the profits of all stores in his region. In other words, if he had three store managers in his region and each manager had an objective of achieving $2 million in profit, the only objective for the regional manager would be the total for all stores, or $6 million. It was suggested to the president that if this were true, there would be no need for a regional manager. If the regional manager was only an "adder-upper," the vice president could just as easily total the profits of all the stores, and one level of management could be eliminated. The president remained adamant in his opinion.

The matter was resolved by drawing up a list of the key-results areas for the total department, without regard for levels of management. The list included:

Sales gross margin	Staffing and training
New store openings	Sales expense
Sales strategy	Market research
Sales tactics	Distribution
Advertising and	Profitability
promotion	Sales policies

Next, the five general guides, listed at the beginning of this chapter, were applied to this list of key-results areas. The following breakdown of key-results areas was arrived at after analysis:

V.P. Store Operations

Profitability (of total operations)
Sales strategy
Sales gross margin
Staffing and training (of regional managers)
Market research
Sales policies

Regional Managers

Sales tactics
Staffing and training (of store managers)
Site selection, new stores

Store Managers

Profitability (of individual stores)
Staffing and training (of store personnel)
Sales expense
Advertising and promotion

Thus, the analysis of key-results areas, by levels, indicated a real need for the regional managers beyond any accountability for the sum of the profits of the store managers reporting to them.

Plant Manager

The manager of a Massachusetts plant in the paper industry is responsible for operating a cost center whose production averages about $20 million in sales volume. Production employees are represented by a strong national union that delegates little autonomy to its lower level officials. Lately, the environmental groups have become increasingly critical of alleged pollution resulting from the plant's operations.

The plant manager began compiling his list of key-results areas by listing all of those for which he could conceivably be held responsible. Initially, his list included:

Operating costs	Labor relations
Operating schedules	Plant safety
Quality assurance	Fixed-asset utilization
Return on capital additions	Training and development
Public relations	of subordinates

Next, he reviewed each of the tentative key-results areas to determine if he should be accountable for them or delegate them down the line. Following this analysis stage, he decided that only a few key-results areas should be retained by him. He retained return on capital additions, fixed-asset utilization, labor relations, public relations, and training and development of subordinates.

The reasons he decided to delegate or retain each of the key-results areas contained in his original list are illustrative of the analysis and priority determination that usually precede delegation:

Operating costs and schedules. He delegated these because they are caused and controlled by lower level managers. Once his subordinates have established objectives for these matters, the plant manager's job is limited to monitoring their progress.

Quality assurance. Here again, the plant manager's role is limited to overall monitoring once the inspection specifications and procedures have been established and a reporting system implemented. The prime accountability for quality rests with the production superintendent and, to a lesser extent, with the foremen.

Return on capital additions. He retained this key-results area because of its significant impact on the performance of the plant as a cost center. Return on capital additions is a prime part of his accountability for capital management, as it exerts a great impact on the return of total assets entrusted to him.

Public relations. Retention of public relations illustrates the importance of priorities. In this case, the plant was coming under increasing fire from the community and the state and federal governments because of the pollution charge. He considered it necessary to maintain a highly centralized approach, at the top level, to present a well-coordinated front to all the plant's critics.

Labor relations. The plant manager retained labor relations because of the highly centralized nature of the union organization. The organization of a company's labor relations approach usually follows the union's organization. Where one is decentralized, so is the other. The same is true of centralization.

Plant safety. Plant safety was delegated for much the same reasons operating costs and schedules were. Lower level managers have prime control over and direction of safety matters. The plant manager monitors; he doesn't execute.

Fixed-asset utilization. The retention of this key-results area, coupled with retention of return on capital additions, gives the plant manager direction and control over his total accountability for capital management. Both require the broad decision making that can only take place at the top level. Capital management requires top-level accountability because of the total organizing, planning, and pursuing of alternatives that must take place.

Training subordinates. His accountability for developing the four subordinates reporting to him could not be delegated because of the highly personal superior-to-subordinate relationship involved. Others may assist him, but this accountability can never be successfully delegated.

Superintendent and Foremen

The division of key-results areas between first-line supervisors and their superior will vary materially, based on many factors. Chief among these is the nature of the manufacturing operation. An integrated manufacturing system, a highly automated automobile assembly line, for example, differs substantially from a job-shop machining operation. Key-results areas by levels will differ accordingly.

The common key-results areas for a superintendent and the foremen reporting to him:

Superintendent	Foremen
Departmental planning and scheduling	Direct labor
	Direct materials
Interdepartmental labor utilization	Reject rates
	Rework
Total manufacturing costs	Supplies
Training and development of foremen	Machines and tools
	Setup time

Prime Versus Final Accountability

For years a popular premise has been that accountability cannot be delegated. If this is true, only the chief executive officer of the corporation has any accountability. Carried one step further, it could be argued that only the board of directors has any accountability, because in the final analysis the board is accountable for everything that goes on in the company. I maintain that it is both possible and necessary for accountability to be delegated. However, to avoid needless debates with classical management thinking, let's view accountability as being of two types: *prime* and *final*.

Prime accountability rests with the manager who must achieve the results. He is nearest the action and the first person from whom the results are expected. He is the delegatee. The manager with final accountability is the delegator—the higher level manager who insures that the action is taken.

In practice, every manager in an organization should be delegated prime accountability for desired results. As we move up the organizational ladder, each superior manager should have prime accountability for matters he will handle himself and final accountability for results to be accomplished by his subordinates.

No manager should limit his accountability to sitting back and adding up the accomplishments of his subordinates. He would become a bookkeeper or monitor, an example of a human being who could be replaced by data processing equipment. The bookkeeper or monitor type of manager has little fun and demonstrates little creativity and ingenuity. Usually, he ends up either abdicating his accountability or, for want of something better to do, spending his day over-controlling or overdirecting his subordinates.

The superior manager can never neglect doing everything possible to insure the achievement of the sum of the accountabilities of his subordinates, but his own accountability goes further. He must have additional accountability in the key-results areas peculiar to his own responsibility.

[11]

AUTHORITY
THAT GETS RESULTS

AUTHORITY IS the essential ingredient of the delegation process, permitting the delegation to be carried out. Regardless of the skill and thoroughness with which the preceding parts of the delegation process have been handled, no delegation takes place if the subordinate is not granted the authority to accomplish his accountability.

It is sometimes said that managers with considerable influence don't require authority and that the less influence a manager has the more authority he needs. Under certain circumstances, there is a grain of truth in this generality. However, it begs the issue. Sound delegation and organizational clarity cannot be based on permitting all an organization's managers to test how much influence they can muster and peddle to their associates. Among other undesirable results, running an organization by influence can quickly result in chaos and the furthering of low-priority matters at the expense of those worthy of a higher priority.

The authority required for effective delegation is characterized by several attributes:

1. There must be a transfer of power from the superior to the subordinate. Authority must be considered synonymous with the power to act.

2. Authority must be specific enough for the subordinate to proceed without fear of exceeding his authority or having his actions reversed. Instances involving the use of poor judgment where consequences would be highly detrimental to the organization would be an exception, of course.

3. Authority should be granted in advance rather than on an ad hoc basis, so that the manager may plan his future course of action more effectively.

4. Authority should be spelled out in writing to facilitate understanding between superior and subordinate and among other managers who may be involved as the delegatee carries out his accountability.

5. Normally, authority should be delegated to the lowest possible organizational level where all information necessary for decision making and action comes together or is available.

6. The authority delegated must be publicized to all persons who may be affected or involved in the action.

7. Above all, the degree of authority must equal the extent of the subordinate's accountability.

Common Mistakes

Although few managers would question the wisdom of the principle that a subordinate must have sufficient authority to perform his job, the principle often is violated in practice. Some of the commoner violations follow.

Commensurate authority. Frequently, the catchall phrase "he enjoys authority commensurate with the job" is used to describe the manager's authority. However, this often becomes a myth in actual practice; the definition is so general that little if any actual authority may be transferred. Quite often the words mean "take the action and I'll let you know whether or not I agree with you." As the word "commensurate" is subjective and means different things to different people, it provides no guidance to anyone. It must be defined in specific terms.

The premise that a manager should enjoy authority commensurate with his job is sound. However, the premise must be translated into practice. It acknowledges the need for authority, with the understanding that additional, more specific, authority grants are forthcoming. These specific grants must be made as early in the game as possible to prevent the manager from proceeding at his own peril or amid confusion. Naturally, the specific authorities granted will be influenced by the competence of the incumbents, the magnitude of the problems they are facing, their accountabilities, and circumstances.

An excellent illustration of the weakness and danger inherent in the words "commensurate authority" involved the labor relations manager who served as chief negotiator for his company for negotiating collective bargaining agreements. In actual practice, the commensurate authority he enjoyed meant that he had full authority to meet with the union and receive and discuss its demands. However, he was required to call headquarters before making any but the most routine concessions. He soon fell into the habit of using this requirement as a crutch and excused himself to "call the boss" whenever negotiations got particularly sticky.

Anyone who has negotiated a labor contract knows that often there comes a time when the contract can be settled then and there. However, if the negotiator is not authorized to settle at that moment of receptivity, the negotiations may drag out for weeks. This particular company negotiator was never able to take advantage of the magic moment. The union representatives knew he was only a messenger boy and instead of being willing to settle, they usually tried to get more. Also, the labor relations manager had no opportunity

139

to plan his strategy and tactics to settle at a particular figure because he never knew what figure headquarters would agree to.

Ratification. As the term implies, ratification involves an after-the-fact approval of an action by the manager's superior. It is undesirable, for at least two reasons, as a means of securing authority. The subordinate proceeds at his own peril without any concrete idea as to whether his boss will approve the action. And the boss is forced to approve the action—frequently by condoning it—or overrule his subordinate. It is eminently better for both parties to have the authority delegated in advance.

Symptomatic of this weakness is the boss who tells his subordinate that it really isn't necessary to spell out specific authority; that the two of them will resolve the authority question as the delegated project proceeds. Very often this type of boss actually is saying that he doesn't want to share his authority or he likes to keep his finger in the pie by having his people constantly check back with him.

Accountability but not authority. Most people are willing to let their subordinates share with them in performing the work; however, a proportionate number are not always willing to give up some of their authority. In other words they want and seek help with the chores but are reluctant to share the power, influence, and status that accompany authority. These reluctant bosses are great developers of followers, but they seldom become known as a leader of leaders; leadership goes with authority.

Authority survives the action. Authority means not only the superior granting it before the action but also the superior supporting it after the action. A president delegated authority to a vice president to replace any department head who was incompetent. The vice president decided a particular department head would have to go. Because of the key nature of the job to the company, the vice president mentioned his plans to the president whose reaction was, "It's your show, use your own judgment." The vice president terminated the substandard department head. However, without informing the vice president, the president contacted the department head and arranged a clandestine meeting with him. Later, the president called in the vice president and proceeded to hint at several reasons he believed the vice president had erred. Subsequently, the vice president was never convinced that he had the authority to run his own show and he checked with the president before making any but the most routine decisions.

The continuing support phase means the superior must (1) make sure the subordinate understands what is expected of him; (2) help the subordinate to reach his objectives by providing information, staff assistance, and tools as needed; and (3) give him advice, counsel, and correction without taking away any part of his accountability and authority.

Authority is personal. Sections of an earlier chapter discussed the personal nature of accountability. As authority must be tailored to accountability, it follows logically that authority also must be personal. It must be based on such differences as accountability, competence, and circumstances surrounding the delegation. A manager operating a plant thousands of miles away in a foreign country will require a different authority from that of his local counterpart, who is only a few miles away from the boss. Standard schedules or manuals of authority can impede the performance of an aggressive manager with ambitious accountability; the same authority would be more than enough for a less qualified manager. Tailoring of authority to match accountability is discussed later in this chapter.

Securing Authorities

Authority usually is spoken of as something the superior grants his subordinates. This thinking places the initiative on the superior's shoulders. For purposes of tailoring authority to accountability it would be better if authority were looked upon as powers recommended by the subordinate to the superior and approved by the latter. This transfers the initiative to the subordinate, where it belongs. How often have we heard a subordinate gripe about his lack of authority and then learn that he has never recommended that his authority be increased?

Subordinate managers would be well advised to keep reminding themselves that they—not their superiors—are most affected by success or failure on their jobs. They must take the initiative in removing any obstacles to performance, including being sure they get all necessary authority.

The boss, as his contribution to setting authorities, must remember that the more latitude he grants his subordinates—both in terms of allowing them to participate in establishing their authority and in the amount of the authority—the more committed and motivated his people will be to do a better job. Once more it's a matter of allowing managers to help determine their own destiny.

Practice of a Billion-Dollar Company

One of the better examples of tailoring authority to accountability is furnished by a company with sales of $1.5 billion in the instrument, controls, and data processing industry. The company operates worldwide and employs about 50,000 people. Operations are organized by corporate divisions headed by division general managers who report to a group executive at headquarters. All authorities are embodied in a corporate authority manual constructed along the following lines.

First, the authorities are determined for all parent corporation officers and the numerous divisional general managers based on their accountabilities. Then these are reduced to writing. Together they constitute the basic authority manual for the corporation as a whole.

Next, the recommended accountabilities are approved

for each manager below the division general manager. Then each subordinate manager recommends the authority he requires for the target period, based on his accountability. Recommended authorities that are approved are reduced to writing. Together they form the division authority manual.

When all authorities have been agreed to, the combined contents of the corporate authority manual and the division manual provide the agreed-upon authorities for all managers from the chief executive officer down to and including the lowest level of management.

It would appear at first glance that sheer size would make it impossible for this company to tailor authorities to individual accountabilities. However, its many years of successful practice provide dramatic proof that a large organization need not fall back on the expediency followed by so many others of assigning standard authorities for each level of management without regard to the differing accountabilities of the various managers even those working at the same level. In many large organizations the authority to approve expenditures is the same for all managers working at the same level; it frequently appears as follows:

Position	Maximum Authority
Vice president	$100,000
Plant manager	50,000
Superintendent	25,000
General foreman	10,000
Foreman	5,000

Expressing Authorities

Once authorities have been decided upon and approved, they must be put in writing and embodied in some form of official document. In order to do this, authorities are categorized. Categories in common use include general authorities, specific authorities, and budgetary authorities.

143

General authorities. This category probably is the least desirable of all unless it is accompanied by limits or parameters that spell out the upper limits of the manager's authority.

General authorities are usually broken down by three degrees and abbreviated with the code letters A, B, and C:

A. Action over which the manager has complete authority. He requires neither prior approval from his superior nor the briefing of his superior after the action.
B. Action the manager may take within specified limits without prior approval of his superior but for which he must report the completed action to his superior.
C. Action which the manager must clear in advance with his superior.

An example of how these codes work in actual practice is illustrated by a manager's authority for handling labor relations. The actions and authority codes are as follows:

Action	Code
Settling grievances that are not likely to be precedent setting	A
Settling grievances that involve departures from past practice	B
Settling grievances where work stoppages or strikes are threatened	C

Authorities derived from policies. Another general form of authority often emanates from policy statements of the organization. These usually are more in the form of guides than authorities and they cover many managers rather than being tailored to the accountability of individuals.

However, these can be tailored somewhat by providing specific exceptions to the policy when it is desirable to do so. Many policies are made in the main office and cover almost everyone in the company. For example, a public relations policy specifies those individuals who may speak for or issue press releases about the company. Other policies cover only a segment of employees, such as a pricing policy for the sales force. Frequently it is desirable to grant exceptions to these policies for certain individuals and particularly for those who may be located some distance from headquarters.

Pricing policies serve as a good example of the use of exceptions. They are usually determined at the highest level in the organization because of the need for close coordination of costs and revenues, inventory levels, economic forecasts, and fair trade and antitrust considerations. Exceptions are then made for the local regional and district managers, who are better equipped to size up such matters as local competition, consumer acceptance, and local buying habits. These exceptions usually are expressed as a permissible range, say 5 percent, within which he may deviate.

Unless these tailored exceptions are made, policies are of limited benefit because they are too general and are usually expressed as constraints on action.

Authorities derived from procedures. Procedures, which usually are formulated to implement policies, can provide a source of additional authority grants for managers. Procedures usually include a more specific type of authority than that provided by policies. A good example is the procedure commonly used to implement and administer a policy regarding the hiring of new employees—especially at the exempt level. The procedure will spell out the responsibility and authority of the personnel representative, the immediate superior of the employee being hired, and higher level managers if the job being manned exceeds a certain salary or job level.

Specific authorities. Whether these authorities are spelled out as part of the manager's statement of accountability or in a separate authority manual is not the important issue. What is important is that these authorities be tailored to the manager's accountability.

Figure 11-1 illustrates the 32 different points covered by the list of authorities for a president. Figure 11-2 illustrates another method of spelling out authorities for seven managerial jobs in a pharmaceuticals-chemicals company.

(*Text continues on page 152.*)

Figure 11-1. Sample list of authorities for the president of a company.

Within the limits of the bylaws and the policies of the board of directors and the authorities reserved by them and the executive committee of the board, the president has full authority to conduct the affairs of the company. His principal authorities are listed below:

Area of Authority	*Authority*
1. Election of directors	None
2. Creation or dissolution of business entities	None
3. Election of officers	None
4. Authorization of employee benefit plans, such as stock options, group insurance, pension, and profit-sharing plans	None
5. Major financing and issuance of securities	None
6. Guarantee of debts or obligations	None
7. Mergers or acquisitions	None
8. Declaration of dividends	None
9. Charitable contributions	Under $2,000
10. Selection of public accountants	None
11. Qualification for doing business or withdrawal from any state, territory, or country	None
12. Mortgaging or pledging assets other than in the ordinary course of business	None
13. Retirement	
a. Deferred retirement	None
b. Supplemental retirement payments	None
14. Approval of annual report to stockholders	None
15. Designation of depositories for company funds and signing authorities	None
16. Hiring, salary, and salary adjustment	Under $25,000

Figure 11-1. (Continued).

17. Termination of personnel (except officers)	Full
18. Transfer of personnel	Full
19. Promotion of personnel	Full
20. Authorizing paid overtime	Full
21. Employing professional services	Full
22. Authorization of travel, and of travel and entertainment expense	Full
23. Union contracts	Full
24. Adjusting hourly wages	Full
25. Approval of extra compensation	None
26. Authorization of expenditures	
a. Real property	None
b. Other capital assets	Under $50,000
c. Equity securities	Under $50,000
d. Research and development	Under $50,000 any one project
e. Leases	Under total rental of $40,000
f. Portfolio, bonds, notes, and certificates	Full
g. Patents, know-how, and rights	Under $30,000 any one project
27. Disposing of assets	
a. Real property	None
b. Other capital assets	Under $20,000
c. Equity securities	Under $15,000
28. Credit arrangements	Full
29. Sales prices of products and services	Full
30. Approving power of attorney	Full
31. Intracompany transfer of funds	Full
32. Public announcements of overall matters	Full

SOURCE: R. C. Smyth, *Financial Incentives for Management* (New York: McGraw-Hill, 1960), pp. 31–32.

Figure 11-2. Authorities for seven executives in a pharmaceuticals-chemicals company.

Subject Area	V.P.[1]	Tech. Dir.	Operat. Serv. Dir.	Prod. Dir.	Sales & Mktg. Dir.	Controller	Dir. of Pers.	Remarks
Employment contracts	U	U	U	U	U	U	U	Subject to joint approval of area head and director of personnel
Collective bargaining agreements	U	—	—	U	—	—	U	
Sales contracts	U	—	—	—	U	—	—	
Research agreements	U	U	—	—	—	—	—	
Consultant agreements	U	U	U	U	U	U	U	
Customs business—importation	U	—	U	—	—	—	—	
Customs brokers	—	—	U	—	—	—	—	
Forwarding agents	—	—	U	—	—	—	—	
Cert. correct, sales invoices	U	—	—	—	U	U	—	
Public bids	U	—	—	—	U	U	—	
Contracts and bonds with governments	U	—	—	—	U	U	—	
Exec. of drafts and endorse B/L	U	—	—	—	U	U	—	
Export and import document endorsements	U	—	U	U	U	U	—	

						Remarks
Narcotics matters	—	—	L (a)	L (b)	U	—	(a) Limited to documents relating to import of narcotics (b) Limited to reports prepared and signed by —— plant personnel
Transportation, traffic, and warehouse	U	—	U	—	—	—	
Real estate leases	L	—	—	—	L	L	Authority may not be redelegated
Releases for injury or damage	U	—	—	—	—	—	
Government applications and reports	U	U	U	—	—	—	
Repair and demolition	$5,000	$5,000	$5,000	$5,000	$5,000	$5,000	
Labeling exemption agreements	—	U	—	—	—	—	
Capital expenditures and sale of assets	$25,000	$10,000	$10,000	$10,000	$5,000	$5,000	
Licensing and use motor vehicles	U	—	—	U	U	—	

U = unlimited authority; — = no authority; L = limited authority (see "Remarks" column).

[1] Acts for division president (with authority identical to the division president) during his absence.

(Continued)

Figure 11-2. (Continued).

Subject Area	V.P.[1]	Tech Dir.	Operat. Serv. Dir.	Prod. Dir.	Sales & Mktg. Dir.	Controller	Dir. of Pers.	Remarks
Requisitions and related matters								
(1) Requisitions, requests for sundry orders	U	U	U	U	U	U	U	
(2) Check vouchers, remittance statements, invoices	$5,000 (a)	$5,000 (b)	$5,000 (c)	$5,000 (d)	$5,000 (e)	$5,000 (f)	$5,000	(a) Unlimited for marine magnesium charges (b) Unlimited for Food and Drug Act testing charges (c) Unlimited for carrier and requisitioned material and service charges (d) Unlimited for fuel, utilities, and cafeteria charges (e) Unlimited for brokerage and commissions (f) Unlimited for payroll entries, purchases by or under purchasing jurisdiction, all other vouchers

(3) Travel advancements—self	$500	$500	$500	$500	$500	$500	$500	
(4) Travel advancements—others	$1,000	$1,000	$1,000	$1,000	$1,000	$1,000	$1,000	
(5) Expense accounts—others	$1,000	$1,000	$1,000	$1,000	$1,000	$1,000	$1,000	Expense accounts, including petty cash vouchers, subject to countersignature by controller or employee designated by him
Purchases, sundry orders, and related matters	U	—	U	L (a)	L (b)	—	—	(a) Items and amounts to be purchased by the plants will be specified by purchasing (b) Limited to purchase of printed and promotional material and exhibit space in unlimited dollar amount within approved budget
Contributions and memberships	$500	$500	$500	$500	$500	$1,000	$500	
Personnel actions	U	U	U	U	U	U	U	Includes authority to approve compensation through grade 15, subject to approval of salary committee

Source: C. L. Bennett, *Defining the Manager's Job* (AMA, 1958), pp. 435–437.

Budgetary authorities. Once approved, a properly prepared budget can act as another source of authority and permit the manager to proceed on his own within the budget limits. This authority may be spelled out as "not to exceed the budget" or "not to exceed the budget by more than 5 percent" without securing advance approval.

The words "properly prepared" are used advisedly. They mean that the budget should be determined after the accountabilities have been approved. Otherwise, the manager ends up with accountabilities tailored to authorities rather than the reverse. It may be a small difference, but it is an all-important one. Too often the budget acts as an unnecessary constraint and limits the manager in exercising his full potential. Every manager should be permitted to exercise every bit of initiative and capability he has when recommending his objectives. Then the control (budget) should be applied. The control shouldn't be determined first, with the manager forced to confine his potential to the control.

To demonstrate the difference in practice, assume a sales manager is required to work within a maximum advertising budget of $20,000. He must work backward to determine how many units of sales this budget will support. His sales volume has been tailored to his authority as spelled out in the budget. His authority may support only 200 units of sales. Let's reverse the procedure and review what can happen when authority is tailored to accountability. In this instance the sales manager determines that he can sell 300 units, justifies the economics involved, and requests an advertising budget of $25,000. The small incremental cost of the additional advertising will be more than recovered by the additional sales. In essence, budgets should reflect plans and sales, not determine them.

Revising Authorities

Whenever authority is granted in advance—and it should be to the maximum extent possible—provision must be made for revising the authority as necessitated by changing circumstances. Plans may not work out as scheduled. Managers may be able to handle more or less authority than was first anticipated.

Methods for revising authorities range from the informal to the formal. In most instances heavy reliance is placed on the subordinate to recommend changes whenever he feels they are needed; this is desirable as it places the initiative on the manager where it belongs. Frequently, changes are initiated by the superior based on his observations.

The more formal approach is practiced by a large company in the floor-covering industry. This company conducts formal quarterly reviews with its managers to review performance as against objectives. During these reviews, a standard item on the agenda is a review of the authority granted to each manager. Thus, each manager knows he will have a minimum of four times in court each year at which he may request changes in his authority.

Regardless of how diligently and how well a company sets the authorities for its managers, situations will develop that are not covered by the delegated authorities. Even the chief executive officer of an organization, the manager with more authority than anyone else, must on occasion turn to his executive committee or the board of directors to resolve questions about his authority.

The goal when establishing authorities should be to cover the preponderance of actions the manager will be required to take. These should be closely tailored to individual accountabilities by providing the subordinate with an active opportunity to recommend the authorities he will require and then approving them before he begins carrying out his job.

The most effective delegation of authority occurs when the subordinate is able to answer all of the following questions in the affirmative:

153

1. Is there at least one written record to which I can refer to determine my authority?
2. Did I participate in establishing my authorities?
3. Are my authorities tailored to my accountabilities?
4. Can I plan ahead to accomplish my accountability with the knowledge that I have the requisite authority?
5. Can I normally act without fear of exceeding my authority or having my action reversed by higher authority?
6. Do my superiors, subordinates, and peers have sufficient knowledge of the authority I enjoy?
7. Has an adequate control and feedback been established—for both my boss's benefit and mine—as to how I am carrying out my authority?

If it is not possible to answer these questions positively, the requisite authority is probably lacking, and the weakness should be remedied before proceeding.

[12]

ESTABLISHING
DYNAMIC CONTROLS

MANY ORGANIZATIONS fail to get full mileage from their control practices because of five fairly common shortcomings. These inadequacies, in turn, exert a major impact on the effectiveness of delegation and any attempt to measure or develop the manager's delegating abilities.

Emphasis on product. The control is designed primarily to calculate product costs and revenues. Its secondary use is as a control on the manager. The emphasis should be reversed. Data collected for the manager's control can be used for determining product costs; the reverse is not equally true.

For example, many accounting systems concentrate on accumulating product costs by including the major cost components, such as materials, labor, overhead, and machinery. This exercise may reflect a total cost of $20 per unit. However, it ignores the many individual managers who had a hand in building up the costs and provides them with little guidance for control purposes.

Control should not be static; it must lead to action. Unfortunately, the word is too deeply rooted in the jargon of management to attempt its removal in a book such as this. However, if control is to be dynamic, its prime purpose must not be to control, to gibe a manager for mistakes, or to embarrass him in his boss's eyes. The real value of controls must be to motivate the manager to action.

Emphasis on wrong level. Too often data are collected for control by the manager's superior rather than primarily for the manager's use. The latter should take precedence; the fallout from data collected and prepared for the manager can be used for control by the superior.

Emphasis not tailored to decision maker. Control should provide for tracking down the source of the decision. For example, the extra costs of producing rush orders often are charged to the production manager, even though the decision to sell and ship the rush items was made by the sales manager. Thus, the control doesn't monitor the production manager's performance but rather the incidence of approved rush orders decided upon by another manager.

Applying specific controls to general matters. Another all-too-common failing is to attempt to apply highly specific controls to general authorities and accountabilities. This is particularly true in organizations in which accountability is not translated into specific objectives. For example, a manager's accountability may be spelled out as "the responsibility for implementing and directing the best community relations." This is very general at best, and the manager's task is subject to many different interpretations. How, then, can a specific control be applied? One of the controls probably will be expressed in terms of the cost of the activities and programs undertaken. However, the cost control will be inadequate because it does not measure return on costs. Proper control should reflect both the costs and the return.

Lack of tailoring. This failure represents one of the real weaknesses in many control procedures or reports. Often the only control reports received by managers in the same organization are highly standard ones covering the same categories—usually costs or revenue. The only difference is in the figures; the column and category headings are all the same. Thus, even though each manager will have different "make or break" aspects inherent in his job, different priorities, and different objectives, an attempt is made to have each manager exert control through a standard report. Tailoring of controls to individual accountabilities is discussed later in this chapter.

Critical Importance of Responsibility Accounting

Much of the inadequacy caused by the five shortcomings can be minimized by the adoption of responsibility accounting. Responsibility accounting assumes significant proportions because of its ability both to motivate managers and to help them control their operations.

Increasingly, practicing businessmen and behavioral scientists are demonstrating that the more achievement-oriented a manager is, the more interested he is in feedback on his performance. Indeed, they have proven that proper feedback is, in itself, a significant motivator. The reasons would appear to be obvious, although not always appreciated. A manager who wants to exert only normal effort and achieve only average results isn't too interested in feedback on his performance. He doesn't want to be reminded how poorly he is doing. He especially doesn't want his boss to have such data. The achievement-oriented manager, on the other hand, sets tough goals for himself and demands feedback to determine how well he is performing. The former manager studiously avoids measurements of his performance; the latter demands them.

Recent studies in Emory Air Freight and other organizations have illustrated significant increases in output resulting from feedback to managers and employees. Conversely, available evidence suggests that an effective way to destroy motivation is to give a person a job to do but not let him know how well or poorly he is doing on the job. The experiences of business for over 40 years with the traditional type of managerial appraisal system—a system that measured personality traits rather than results—have undoubtedly proven that the lack of meaningful feedback to the manager was one of the real reasons the system failed miserably as a motivator of better performance.

However, if responsibility accounting is to serve its dual role of motivation and control, it must be truly individual in nature. It must be tailored to report or feed data back to the individual manager, not to a group of managers or the manager's superior. It must reflect his performance against his individual accountability. It should be based on matters over which he has control, not matters whose destiny is determined by someone else.

Management by Exception

Management by exception is highly compatible with, and supportive to, proper delegation. It permits the manager to control his operation with a minimum of effort and helps him to avoid overcontrol—giving too much attention to managers or operations that are proceeding smoothly.

Prerequisites. Two absolute prerequisites must be met before management by exception can be practiced effectively: (1) Priorities must be determined, and (2) controls must be established. Both steps are considered prerequisites because a manager cannot concentrate his time and efforts on the most important matters until and unless he knows what they are (priorities) and establishes some method for keeping himself informed as to how well or poorly these important matters are progressing (control).

Determining priorities. The first step in determining priorities is to decide on a practical, meaningful definition of what they are. Many managers use the word to mean any and all activities that must be completed in order to earn a profit. In their eyes, the word is synonymous with "germane" or "necessary." The serious flaw in this definition is that it doesn't give the required attention to the relative importance of each activity, and thus provides no basis for determining in what order each activity should be undertaken.

If the definition of priorities is to be practical and viable, it must provide the manager with a sense of the relative importance to the company's betterment of each task or project, and a guide to the time span in which the task should be completed. Therefore, to the manager, priorities revolve around matters having the highest payback to the company, solutions to the most pressing problems that would stand in the way of realizing the highest paybacks, and identification of the real make-or-break aspects of the business.

Like many other parts of the management process, determination of priorities must begin at the very top. All management personnel must be able to concentrate their efforts to help insure that the company as a whole achieves the highest payback. The first step is to analyze the entire company's posture and to determine what particular factors are most important to the company at that time, according to the particular conditions the company will be facing during the specific time period selected and for which priorities are being determined. Also to be taken into consideration is whether the particular priorities are for a short-range or long-range plan. In making this determination, the company is, in effect, isolating the factors that are critical to its operation. Each company has these critical factors, regardless of its size, industry, or product.

For example, the first and most pressing problem for a company with little, if any, available capital and low profitability might be to earn an immediate profit, possibly even at the expense of earning higher profits in subsequent years. In a capital-heavy company whose earnings are satisfactory, the primary emphasis is usually on greater profits over the long term rather than on immediate profits. In a food drive-in company, the emphasis must be placed on the cost of food sold; factors such as advertising and construction are of far less importance. In an airline company, the priorities are equipment and labor costs.

Just as priorities differ between and among companies, they vary between and among departments within one company. Components of profit and revenue that are important to a sales department do not have the same importance to the production operation. In like fashion, the purchasing and engineering functions have different make-or-break items, as do the personnel department and the research department. Thus, even though the overall priorities of the company must be established by top management, every manager in the company, at every level, bears a responsibility for determining the priorities for the operations under his direction.

Role of finance. The financial department plays a significant role in helping other managers to determine their priorities. Too often, however, this role is not appreciated, and is even neglected, by other managers. Some operating managers regard financial people as busybodies anxious to stick their noses into operations. At best, these managers regard finance as having an after-the-fact role, limited to reporting what has happened after it happens.

To determine priorities properly, a truly joint effort must be made by the operating manager and the financial manager, since each has specialized training and experience that must be brought to bear. The operating manager knows the details and techniques of his operation intimately, but he is not and should not be a qualified financial manager. On the other hand, the financial manager is an expert in all phases of finance, but he is not and should not be an operating manager. By combining their talents, they can impose a real intelligence on the determination of priorities and on the subsequent establishment of controls to monitor the priorities as they unfold in action.

The impact of this joint effort can be illustrated with actual examples. A production manager knows the ins and outs of the production process completely. He is aware of the impact of transferring five additional employees to complete an operation, but he does not know that such a transfer will make the company's costs noncompetitive, a fact well known by the financial officer. In contrast, the financial manager is capable of pricing out any changes in the components of cost, such as the changes in per-unit costs brought about by volume increases. What might appear to be a loss to the operating manager might well be a profit to the financial manager because of the interactions and interrelationships of the numbers. After all, the financial manager is better equipped to decide matters such as the effect of volume on costs and profits, the profit impact of a change in product mix, the cost difference between two methods of operation, and the economics of shifting from one type of production process to another. The production manager must provide the financial man with the operating details of the manpower, product, and equipment involved in decreasing or increasing volume, in switching the product mix, or in changing from one type of production process to another. Neither can manage without the other. Together they make a great team.

Tailoring Controls

Delegation becomes more effective when a continuous tailoring process is followed. Just as accountability must be tailored to responsibility and authority to accountability, control must be tailored to the authority granted. Earlier chapters described the manner in which authorities are tailored to accountability. The final step is to tailor specific controls to the authority.

Controlling major objectives. Once the manager's accountability has been expressed in terms of objectives, the next step consists of establishing controls over these objectives so that the manager (and to a lesser extent his superior) will be able to determine, at any one point in time, exactly how well he is doing in comparison with where he should be at that point. When priorities have been set and the company and all its managers have decided where they want to go, the next step is to tailor the controls or monitoring devices to measure whether or not they are getting there. This is the control function of a manager's job.

Priorities should be expressed in terms of objectives: to earn 10 percent on shareholders' equity, to increase yield of apple-growing operation from 10 to 12 percent, to increase earnings per share from $2.50 to $2.75, and to reduce cost of purchasing a certain component from $1.50 to $1.30 per unit. The next step involves the establishment of controls on these objectives.

Take, for example, an objective for lowering the production reject rate by 10 percent. Before a proper control can be established for this objective, several questions must be resolved: How will progress toward the objective be measured? How often should it be measured? To whom will the measuring reports be sent? What form should the reports take?

Measure. It is of paramount importance here to select the one measure that best describes how well the objective has been accomplished. This requires considerable analysis. Our objective of lowering the reject rate raises several questions. What do we mean by lowering the reject rate? Do we mean units of products, costs, or both? If we mean costs, what costs should be included in measuring accomplishment compared with objective? Must a distinction be made between rejects that must be scrapped and those that can be reworked? What basis do we use for costing out the two categories? The analysis and subsequent answering of questions like these not only helps to determine the best measurement but also frequently helps to improve the structure of the objective itself.

In the case under consideration, the objective is the reduction of reject costs by 10 percent over 1973. The measure can be stated as the total cost of direct materials and labor for units that cannot be reworked, plus total labor costs for reworking all units that can be reworked.

Frequency. Next in terms of proper control is the necessity for determining how frequently measurements should be made. For highly critical matters like sales revenue, measurements may be needed at short intervals, such as semi-weekly or weekly. For other matters, like costs, a weekly report may suffice. Some reports will be much less frequent. In any case, the key to determining the frequency with which a report should be made must be based on two questions. How soon can the data be properly assembled? How soon is the information needed in order to make management decisions?

In our continuing example, let's assume the product involves high material costs and demand is outpacing the ability to produce. Both dictate a high priority on feedback. A decision is made to issue the report on a daily basis, at least until the desired reject level is achieved and is being maintained. Now to the objective and the measure in the tailored control procedure, we add the frequency, which is daily.

Who receives reports? The question of who should receive the reports is rather easily resolved. Management need only determine who needs the report in order to perform his job or to help carry out the objective. If left to his own, every manager in the company would undoubtedly like to receive a copy of the report; status symbols are made of such things. Reports should not be prepared or distributed to promote status. Their purpose is to provide the proper information to the people who require it for decision-making purposes. If a manager needs a copy of the report to perform his job, he should receive it. It not, he shouldn't, because it only compounds paperwork and results in too many cooks. In our continuing objective, let's assume that thorough analysis has determined that only the production manager, the foreman over the operation, the sales manager, the quality assurance manager, and the financial manager require the information in order to perform their jobs. Now the fully tailored control procedure includes the objective, the measure, the frequency of issuance, and the distribution of the report.

Form of report. A decision should be made as to what form the report will take. Will an oral statement suffice? If not, is a special-purpose report required, or is the information included in a report that is already being issued? Once a decision has been made, the control procedure should spell out the name and number of the report by which the information will be transmitted and the person or department responsible for initiating it. Additional examples of tailoring controls to objectives are given in Table 12-1.

Dynamic Control in Action

Two cases illustrate the key role played by dynamic controls in effecting better delegation and management. The executive vice president of a food company became hopelessly bogged down in the details and coordination of the six vice presidents who reported to him. Many of his discussions with his six officers centered around the details of their operations. Often these discussions were generated by the voluminous amount of detailed information on operations all seven officers received. Finally, the executive vice president had a new feedback system installed that emphasized the tailoring of feedback to the individual managers up and down the line. Neither the executive vice president nor the president received the details that had burdened them in the past. They began concentrating their efforts on major problems and opportunities. The executive vice president began operating as a true top executive rather than a policeman over details.

Similar benefits from tailored feedback accrued to a company in the hardware manufacturing business. Historically the foremen had been reluctant to assume the desired

Table 12-1. Examples of tailoring controls to various objectives.

OBJECTIVE *	MEASURE †	FREQUENCY	DISTRIBUTION
Increase yield from apple orchard by 8 percent	Bushels per acre of *salable* fruit	Weekly	Orchard manager Sales manager Financial manager General manager
Reduce customer complaints by a minimum of 5 percent	Number of *written* complaints received which laboratory determines are *valid*	Monthly	Customer service manager Testing laboratory Sales manager
Increase return on investment by 2 percent	*Pretax* earnings on *total assets employed*	Quarterly	President Financial vice president Group vice presidents Board of directors
Reduce total labor costs on operation A by 4 percent	Total *direct* and *indirect* labor costs on a *flexible* budget basis	Weekly	Foreman Superintendent Financial manager
Increase participation of volunteer workers by minimum of 10 percent	Numbers of *eligible* workers who average at least *5 hours per week* or more	Quarterly	Local manager Area manager Executive director

* The objective expresses desired achievements.
† The measure defines and clarifies the intent. The italic words become the key to measuring. If they are changed or omitted, the measure is changed completely. For example, in the apple orchard objective, the word *salable* becomes all important. If it is omitted, then all fruit will be counted when measuring achievement of the objective. When it is included, only fruit meeting sales specifications will count toward the objective.

amount of responsibility for their operations. An analysis indicated that most of the operational reports were designed for, and sent to, the superintendents to whom the foremen reported. The superintendents would review the reports and then discuss any necessary action with the foremen. The initiative for taking corrective action clearly rested with the superintendents, not with the foremen who were in charge.

A complete change was made in the feedback system. Reports were redesigned to meet the needs of the foremen. They were distributed to the foremen with only summary reports going to the superintendents. It was made clear to the foremen that the initiative for acting upon the reports rested with them. Within approximately six months a dramatic change was noticeable in the attitudes of the foremen. They started acting as if they were truly in charge of their operations.

Control of routine objectives. Sometimes routine objectives are basic to the job. (An earlier chapter recommended the use of caution when requiring objectives covering routine parts of the manager's job.) How should they be measured? The most appropriate method for evaluating whether or not an individual has achieved them is to insure that he is aware of the objectives. The manager must tell the subordinate, early in the relationship, what the activities of the job are and what the desired level of performance is. Evaluation should only follow a previous discussion of criteria.

At the same time that the criteria are being made specific, acceptable tolerance limits should be developed. Measurement of the routine should be a major part of the objectives process, but it is of most concern when performance falls outside acceptable levels. Essentially, we are proposing that minimum performance levels be set for routine activities. *Evaluation of routine goals should be by exception, or when these standards are not met.*

Naturally, the ability to manage by exception demands good plans or clear standards from which exceptions can be specified in advance. Odiorne cites the following example:

The paymaster, for example, may report that his routine duties cluster around getting the weekly payroll out every Friday. It is agreed that the measure of exception will be zero—in other words, the boss should expect no exceptions to the diligent performance of this routine duty. Thus, the failure any week to produce the payroll on Friday will be considered an exception that calls for explanation by the subordinate. If the cause were reasonably under his control or could have been averted by extra care or effort, the absence of the payroll will be considered a failure on the part of the subordinate.[1]

The company that truly tailors its controls and practices management by exception is several leagues ahead of the company that does not. It has correctly labeled its priority (make or break) matters, and it has made a distinct separation between these and relatively less important items. Once the priority matters have been segregated and the proper control established to track them, management can concentrate its priority thinking and attention on them. It will not waste its time on a mixture of gold nuggets and iron ore, as other companies might.

This control mechanism has three major benefits for the corporation. First, it enables the manager to schedule his day-to-day activities in a way that permits him to make his maximum contribution, because he knows where he should concentrate his time. Second, it forces him to become intimately familiar with his accountabilities, because management by exception and control cannot be practiced until the manager has singled out the critical aspects of the operation. Third, once the control mechanism is decided upon and set, the manager knows he will receive the earliest possible warning if something goes wrong with his operations. With priorities determined and controls established, it is possible to practice management by exception. The manager can proceed with comfort in the knowledge that he is concentrating on priority matters and has the necessary control over his accountability.

[1] G. L. Odiorne, *Management by Objectives* (New York: Pitman, 1964), p. 104.

167

[13]

DELEGATION AND DECISION MAKING

MANAGEMENT IS decision making and managers must make decisions. The decision-making process is the real guts of both managing and delegation. In fact, one of the better definitions of delegation is "giving others the right to make your decisions." No matter how much accountability and authority are transferred from one person to another, no delegation takes place if the latter cannot or will not make decisions. When lack of decision making occurs, the incumbent becomes a poor manager, an errand boy for someone else, an administrator of another person's dictates, or all three.

Consider the purchasing director who is supposed to be accountable for the cost of purchasing, among other objectives. He must be delegated considerable latitude to make decisions affecting costs as long as they don't interfere with agreed-upon specifications and delivery dates. In actual practice, however, his boss and other executives in the organization dictate which brand-name products to buy and the vendor firm from which they are to be purchased, assign unrealistic delivery dates, set unrealistic product performance standards, insist upon multiple bids when only a couple of vendors can meet the specifications, and set false quality standards. These practices remove many of the areas of the most promising decisions from the purchasing director. He becomes a mere placer of orders or, at best, a buyer. It's a misnomer to call him a purchasing director; he directs little except the processing of purchase requisitions and orders.

Causes of Poor Decision Making

Many factors, other than the incompetence of a manager, can contribute to poor decision making. Often, improper or inadequate delegation is the culprit in the form of:

1. Confused responsibility and accountability
2. Lack of authority or vague authority
3. Inadequate or inaccurate data
4. Poor management atmosphere
5. Failure to set a time limit

Confused Responsibility

It is a well-established fact that on the average a significant area of confusion, often ranging up to 25 percent, exists between the superior and subordinate as to what the subordinate's true responsibility and accountability really are. This is especially true when the decision involves more than one manager or more than one department.

Ford and Bursk outline the dimensions of the problem.[1] First, despite organizational charts that define responsibility areas, many decisions involve several people and depart-

---

[1] Charles H. Ford and E. C. Bursk, "Organizing for Faster Decisions," *Management Review* (April 1971), pp. 4–15.

ments, all of whom have an interest in the decision as it affects their functions. This overlapping of interests and the problems of coordination frequently becloud the identity of the individual who will make the decision.

For example, a decision affecting both sales and production, such as the revision of an existing product, requires coordination between the two departments and generally the acceptance of the decision by each. The problem can be further complicated when there is more than one individual involved within each department. If resolution of their differences is involved, the decision-making power is split even further. When more than two departments are involved, the decision can bounce around indeterminately waiting for someone to make it.

Even if the responsibility for making the decision is clear-cut, when several people and departments are involved, unanimity of agreement is seldom achievable. People tend to feel uncomfortable and to shy away from making a decision in an atmosphere of conflict. The decision is dragged out while the decision maker hopes that somehow unanimity eventually will be achieved. Generally this situation continues until a crisis forces the decision to be made.

Lack of Authority

Often a manager is reluctant to make a decision because he doesn't know what his authority is. May he make the decision or not? If he does, will he be chastised for going too far, especially if the result isn't exactly what was expected? Indecisiveness frequently takes over. The result may be a costly delay in making the decision or no decision at all (management by default).

In addition, the gun-shy decision maker frequently has the responsibility for a decision without the necessary authority to pull all the components together on time. He cannot get the proper and necessary support from other levels of management to permit him to make the decision. The principle of responsibility with commensurate authority is often a myth in practice. The decision awaits the convenience of others who feel no urgency, because the responsibility for making the decision is not theirs.

Factionalism, zealous guarding of departmental prerogatives, and the fact that authority to make a decision is often vested in a person who is remote from the problem and does not feel the same urgency someone closer to it will—all cause the decision to drift. The decision maker will address himself to problems with which he is more directly concerned or more familiar, but which may be less important or pressing to the company than the one he neglects.

The lack of clearly specified authority acts as a crutch for the weak manager who doesn't want to make decisions. He can always toss the matter upstairs for a decision and still be immune from criticism because his authority was not clear. He is provided with a ready-made excuse and a tree to hide behind.

Inadequate Data

Prompt, timely, and accurate data are prerequisites for effective decision making and for measuring the adequacy of the action following the decision. A foreman who is accountable for labor utilization will not be able to handle this delegation unless he is provided with the costs of the various labor components of his operation. For example, before assigning four men to a job, he must know what his labor costs will be and have some standard against which he can compare these costs. Otherwise, he is quite likely to assign five or six men to the job, particularly if it has some priority attached to it. Little purpose is served from telling him his labor costs were too high after the fact. The job has been completed and there is nothing he can do about it. His performance suffers because he doesn't have before-the-fact data on costs and acceptable standards.

The same fate will be suffered by any manager who

wants to do a good job but doesn't have the tools with which to do it. On the other hand, the same void will protect and provide excuses for the weak manager.

Poor Management Atmosphere

Probably few things are more detrimental to decision making than an atmosphere that breeds fear of making a wrong decision. One of the privileges a competent manager must enjoy is the right to be wrong. Although his overall performance will be measured on the number of correct decisions he makes, and their impact on progress, no successful manager can boast with justification that all his decisions have been 100 percent correct.

The key to delegation as it regards decision making is how the matter is handled when a decision doesn't work out as it should. Any manager can give his subordinate a pat on the back when a decision goes well. The critical question is how he handles the subordinate when he doesn't hit a home run in his decision making. If each wrong decision is treated as a major catastrophe and the manager who made it is held up for ridicule, he and other managers will be understandably and increasingly reluctant to make decisions in the future. If, however, mistakes are accepted as events that happen from time to time to any manager with initiative, and they are handled in constructive fashion when they do occur, decision making is enhanced.

Time Limits

Another common cause of poor decision making is the failure to set target dates or times by which an action must be taken. The decision making often drifts and sometimes gets completely lost in the press of other matters. One major advantage of management by objectives or results is its built-in method of setting target times both for major objectives and for subactions under the major objectives.

Any management approach must provide for setting a target time for all major decisions, particularly when more than one manager or department is involved and a decision by one manager must precede a decision by another manager. A "decision tree" or PERT exercise is not recommended for every decision, but some method must be observed for scheduling and time limiting the more important decisions.

Use of Committees

Few managers give high points to the use of committees for decision making, as evidenced by the trite old definition of a camel as a horse that was put together by a committee. However, most of the criticism probably stems from a failure to understand the proper function of a committee in the decision-making process.

The rightful role of a committee, whether it is called together in formal session or is a group with whom the manager checks on an individual, less formal, basis, should be one of information gathering and analysis, plus coordination. Its work is performed prior to the decision and is preparatory to the decision. The decision can then be made by the manager accountable for the action, using the committee work as one of his inputs.

Problems arise when either the committee or the manager attempts to confuse these roles. I once served on an inside board of directors which over a period of time many senior managers began to use as a means to avoid decision making on their own. A board meeting was hastily called whenever anyone brought up a problem. The meeting continued in session until one of its members, any one of them, took a strong position on the issue. A consensus decision usually followed. The managers became weaker and weaker at decision making and stronger and stronger at avoiding accountability. This is an excellent example of misuse of committees and the primary reason they have fallen into disrepute.

The effective manager will make increased use of committees but he'll utilize them in their proper perspective. A couple of profound reasons account for the need for their increased use. The information explosion has made it more and more difficult for one individual to collect and analyze all the information and data that should be brought to bear on a subject. The business atmosphere requires more explicit goals and increasingly sophisticated analyses of alternatives. Also, managers are becoming more convinced that other managers feel a greater sense of commitment to the decision if they have shared in the preparatory work leading to the decision. Committees, properly used, can play a significant role in these regards, as can the organization's technical staff.

Role of Technical Staff

The prime role of the staff department (systems, data processing, marketing, personnel, and so on) in corporate decision making is to make the study upon which management must make its decision. To fulfill this function properly, a good study must do the following:

1. Define the problem clearly.
2. Define and rank possible solutions. Informally define alternative actions into three categories—likely solutions for which analysis will be done in detail; acceptable solutions for which enough analysis will be done to allow management to ask for more facts intelligently; rejected solutions with a short reason each was rejected.
3. Gather all the facts. Report clearly the tangible dollar cost of each solution. Beyond costs, objectively state all tangible but nonfiscal facts that are pertinent. For example, what department heads think of possible solu-

tions, what competitors are doing, management capabilities required to carry out a possible solution.

4. Provide a schedule for suggested solutions.

5. Define clearly all intangible items management must consider (obvious, but not easy to do).

6. State all negative factors.

7. Recommend *one* solution.

This and similar approaches to a staff study seem obvious, but are not often so clearly organized or practiced in corporations. The above is one of many organized ways to give facts to top management. The skill in preparing the facts for top management rests on two factors of implementation: thoroughness in determining, defining, handling, and presenting the facts; and a conceptual understanding of the role of the staff department.

Decision Analysis

Prior to delegating decision-making authority, it is usually advisable to analyze the impact of the various characteristics a decision may entail. This commonly is referred to as decision analysis. Its purpose is to establish the kind of decisions that should be made, at what organization level they should be made, which managers should participate in the decision making, and which managers should be informed after the decisions are made. Again, the needs and objectives of the company are the paramount consideration.

In deciding on the importance and coordination requirements of a decision four major criteria should be considered:

1. The degree of futurity in the decision (How long does it commit the company to a particular course of action? How quickly can this decision be reversed?). In general, the greater the futurity of the decision, the higher in the organization the decision should be made.

2. The impact a decision has on the company or on

other organizational units. Decisions must be made at a level high enough to insure that all affected areas or functions are taken into account.

3. Whether the decisions are recurrent, rare, or unique in nature. Repetitive decisions can be handled within the policy framework; other decisions, whether infrequent or one of a kind, require special handling.

4. The number of qualitative factors that enter into the decision. When qualitative factors (such as are contained in the statements of philosophy and many parts of the environmental analysis) are a significant consideration in the decision-making process, the decision should generally be made at the higher management levels.

Authority for making specified types of decisions should be part of the statement of authority delegated to each position, and responsibility for consulting before or informing after the specified decisions are made should be part of the responsibility statement.

Testing Decision-Making Power

One of the critical tests of the degree of delegation that has taken place is the level of management at which a decision is made. If complete delegation has taken place, the decision will have been made at the lowest level at which all the information necessary for the decision came together. The higher the decision is made, above the point at which the information came together, the less delegation takes place.

For example, a foreman in a manufacturing plant normally is responsible for the labor costs resulting from his expertise in utilizing the employees assigned to him. If, however, the superintendent or general foreman to whom he reports actually makes the assignments either to or within the department, the actual decision-making locus for labor costs has been moved up one level above the foreman. The foreman can only act as a "production pusher" and try to keep his workers busy on their jobs.

In complete delegation, the decision will be made by the person most intimately familiar with the details of the operation concerned; that is, the first level of management with direct control over the operation. Consider a company in which the manufacturing manager normally makes the decisions regarding production scheduling and costs. An influential customer phones the executive vice president directly and demands a rush order on a large shipment. The latter agrees to ship it by a certain date. He has failed the delegation test. Decision making has not been delegated to the manufacturing manager, the man closest to the action and most familiar with it.

Another effective technique can guide a manager in determining how much delegation has taken place at lower levels in his department. He should select a fairly routine subject and then telephone a subordinate two or three levels down the line—the subordinate supposedly responsible—and pose a question on that subject. If the subordinate says that he must check with his boss and return the call, or if his boss returns the call, there is a legitimate question about how much delegation has taken place. Is the subordinate empowered to make decisions?

Each of these tests assumes that the manager in question is receiving the data that would be provided by a well-functioning responsibility accounting system.

Steps in Positive Decision Making

For management to delegate authority and provide an atmosphere for decisive decision making is no clarion call for undisciplined decision making. Management must realize that decisive, unafraid executives sometimes need more management and support than the timid. It is time to retune the decision-making apparatus to the more competitive atmosphere of the next decade. Paradoxically, tomorrow's management demands imagination, flexibility, decisiveness, and innovation; today's management often is heading in the opposite direction.

Specific steps are necessary to rekindle the decision-making process:

1. Recognize the problem and get your superiors and subordinates to develop a sense of urgency rather than procrastination. Undoubtedly you need the soft sell to do this unless you are the chief.

2. When major decisions are made, make it clear why they were made, why other alternatives were not chosen, what can go wrong, how great the risk for error was at the time the decision was made, and what future factors could cause problems with today's decisions. ("If the Government raises interest rates, our decision to form a Homebuilding Division should be reevaluated.") Get reasons for major decisions on paper. This can lead to an accusation of "Alibi Paper," but this is preferable to executive timidity.

3. Continually review major decisions, and do not be afraid to suggest changes to old decisions if changing conditions dictate new decisions.

4. Introduce a policy of time limits even for routine decisions and enforce the policy.

5. Give the person closest to the problem the responsibility to implement major decisions and give him the authority to make required "subdecisions." Make available any help he needs both up and down the chain of command.

6. Develop a mistake sharing and credit sharing attitude by requiring those who provide the decision maker with information to say what they would do if the decision was theirs. The answers will often run the gamut from A to Z, but the decison maker will avoid executive myopia by getting many opinions to consider. "A prince," Machiavelli wrote, "should be a great asker of questions."

7. Reward the decision maker. Salary increases and promotions to the aggressive manager will provide a spur to the timid.

8. Give people more training in areas with which they are too unfamiliar to decide between conflicting views of experts.

9. Refine the organization table so responsibility for decisions, even those involving several departments, rest with one man. Be

tolerant of mistakes and miscalculation. All good decision makers make mistakes. Of course, a baseball big leaguer will get sent to the minors for batting .200 over a season. Hopefully, this won't happen for striking out once in a crucial situation.[2]

Decisions enjoy various levels of commitment to carrying them out. One reason is the degree to which the support of the appropriate managers can be gained and maintained. Countless managers have found that their commitment and motivation to any endeavor—especially the execution of decisions—will vary according to how effective a voice they had in determining the action. An effective voice means a full opportunity to express recommendations and to give substantiating reasons before a receptive, attentive audience and to debate contrary views and recommendations, including those of his boss, fully.

Traditionally, management theory has held that a decision should be made by the manager accountable for executing it. It is time for translating theory into practice. There is little to be gained from a decision that embodies the ultimate in wisdom and foresight if the decision falls by the wayside in execution.

An otherwise great decision may suffer in execution if it is made almost exclusively by someone other than the managers who must carry it out. In contrast, a similar decision, even if not as well made, may bring spectacular results when the managers involved in executing it had a major voice in making it. Delegation, which emphasizes truly decentralized decision making, has much to recommend it for those who would optimize the results flowing from decisions.

[2] Alvin Borenstine, "The Theory and Practice of Decision Making on the Firing Line," unpublished paper presented at 1971 International Systems meeting.

[14]

DEVELOPING MANAGERS THROUGH DELEGATION

OF ALL THE disasters that can befall a manager none is more serious than for him to find himself in a position in which he has already been where he's going. Instead of receiving a year of experience each year, he merely puts in another year of the same experience. Helping the manager to avoid stagnation should be the real purpose of any development activity.

The rationale of development activity is summarized by a rather homely, but valid, description: If I catch a fish for you, it will feed you for one meal. If I can help to teach you to catch your own fish, you can feed yourself forever. The former involves no delegation and no development. The latter contemplates development through delegation.

The key to the role delegation plays in developing managers hinges on understanding how development takes place. Contrary to a popular misconception, a superior does not develop a subordinate. He may provide the subordinate with the opportunity, assistance, and vehicles for development, but the subordinate must develop himself. No one can do it for him.

In the early 1950s, a research project conducted by General Electric Company culminated in a list of principles for realizing maximum benefit from developmental programs. Seven of these principles are of special significance to development through delegation:

1. The development process is a highly individual matter. People cannot be developed by means of canned, cut-and-dried, over-standardized methods.

2. Every man's development is self-development. Development is not something you do "to" a man. It's something he does for himself.

3. The development of people cannot be based upon any set of ideal or specified personality characteristics or traits. Equally effective managers may have different strengths and weaknesses.

4. A man's development is 90 percent the result of his experience in his day-to-day work.

5. Primary emphasis must be on development in the present assignment, rather than emphasis on a promotional ladder.

6. Decentralization of decision making is a prime instrument of development.

7. A man's immediate line superior is responsible for the people who work under his direction. Staff experts such as personnel and training specialists can help but they cannot replace the immediate superior.[1]

No recognized authority has quarreled with these findings since they were made.

Impact on Development

These principles, when applied to delegation, can be boiled down to at least two major requirements. One must be met by the superior and one by the subordinate:

[1] Moorhead Wright, "Individual Growth: The Basic Principles," *Personnel* (September–October 1960).

1. The superior must provide the opportunity for development to take place and provide an atmosphere conducive to it taking place.
2. The subordinate must accept strict accountability and be willing and competent to stand on his own two feet in carrying out his accountability.

If improper delegation results from the failure of either party to meet his requirement, the effectiveness of the development process will be lessened. Delegating for development should make each manager in the organization, regardless of his level or accountability, believe and act as if he were chief executive officer of his own little "company" within the bigger company. He should look upon each problem and opportunity within his unit as being his alone, to solve or capitalize on before he turns to his boss or others for advice or assistance. He may benefit from information inputs from staff experts and other associates, but the final accountability for the problem or opportunity is his.

Delegation Is Essential

The old saw that no one ever learned to swim without getting in the water has particular application to developing managers. Indeed, development cannot take place in the absence of delegation, a point well illustrated by pilot training.

Pilots usually are trained in two separate phases—ground school and flight training. The ground-school phase comprises studying subjects like navigation, weather, and the principles of flight. Many students can master all of these and, on paper, they would be rated excellent pilots. However, many of the "great on paper" students never make it beyond the first few hours of instruction.

The real test takes place when the instructor climbs out of the plane and tells the student to take his first solo flight. For the first time since he began his training, the student has real accountability he alone must handle. He no longer will have an instructor with him to whom he can turn if a question develops. He no longer can take comfort in the knowledge that the instructor will compensate for any mistake he may make. He will be alone to solve his own problems. He will start to develop and grow as the manager in charge of the operation. His mettle will be tested thoroughly, which would not happen as long as the instructor was present to rely on.

The loneliest time in the world for the student pilot occurs when he hears the instructor's words, "Okay, take it around once by yourself." Managers must experience the same lonely time before they can start to develop effectively. The superior must make certain this lonely time takes place.

Develop, Don't Baby

The fine line that often exists between developing a man and babying him is illustrated by the father who was anxious to instill in his son the value of earning his own money. He encouraged his son to get a job delivering newspapers before school each morning. The son became a route carrier. But so did the father.

The father usually found some excuse to drive his son around the route each morning. He told him when to collect payments from the customers and helped to maintain the collection books. He participated in decisions on many detailed questions concerning the route, including what portion of each week's earnings the son should put in his savings account. Customers on the route began phoning the father whenever the delivery was late or they didn't receive a paper.

One day, the father asked the son's boss how the son was doing on his paper route. The boss said, "I can't tell you how well your son is doing, but you seem to be doing a great job and together you and your son are one of our top carriers." The comments of the boss are well taken. The son had never been allowed to assume accountability for the route; his development was debatable at best. Also, the results were achieved by the combined efforts of both father and son; the son's real contribution could not be measured.

This example can be translated into a managerial context. It shows mistakes commonly made when delegating; namely, overdirecting, not permitting the subordinate to stand on his own feet and solve his own problems, not permitting him to do his own planning and execution, and a confusion of accountability for results. How often do we encounter situations in which it is impossible to determine whether the superior, the subordinate, or both are responsible for the subordinate's results or lack of results?

Develop Through Problem Solving

Early in my career I was an assistant to an extremely capable department head. During the department head's absences he delegated accountability to me for running the department. Everything always went quite smoothly when he was around. However, a problem requiring more than routine decisions would usually develop when he was away. In the beginning, attempts were made to telephone him, but he was seldom available. I began to question just how good a manager he was. His planning ability seemed to be lacking because problems always cropped up when he went away, and he was not available for consultation. Gradually I became more adept at dealing with the problems and felt more comfortable when they came up. Three years later the boss was promoted and I became the department head.

Years later—after having often observed how the boss handled all his subordinates—I wasn't too surprised to learn that the problems that developed and the unavailability of the boss were not accidental or caused by lack of planning. They were an integral part of the boss's concerted plans for developing his subordinates.

Don't Develop from Confusion

Burt K. Scanlon, professor of management at the University of Oklahoma, told me this example. After leaving the university, Ken Rawlins was employed as a production planning and control specialist in a large manufacturing concern. He spent one year on the job, had become disillusioned, and was considering resigning. His superior was a man of considerable experience with a great deal of technical know-how. Herein lay the problem. Ken's job was essentially that of a clerk. He compiled production data and summarized them in reports of various kinds. These reports were submitted to his superior. If and when they revealed problems in meeting schedules or quality requirements the follow-up action was also initiated by his boss. On several occasions (in his desire to add depth to the job), Ken suggested he might follow through on a project. He was always rebuffed with the comment "Maybe some other time, we have to keep up on the paperwork." Needless to say, the department's operation was quite hectic. Crises were an everyday occurrence since the department manager spent more time doing than managing.

Finally, the situation reached a point of no return and a new manager took over. Ken's initial reaction was to play it close to the vest, doing just what was asked in terms of compiling data. About the second week Ken submitted a report showing some serious discrepancies between the production plan and what was actually occurring. When asked what he proposed to do about it by way of follow-up to uncover the problem, Ken explained that he hadn't given it any thought since he saw his job as one of just compiling the data. The new manager suggested that perhaps the scope of Ken's job had been too narrow in the past and that it should be expanded both for his own benefit and for that of the department and the company.

Together Ken and his superior explored possible problem areas, a strategy to investigate these possibilities, and a timetable to solve the problem he had uncovered. Within these broad limits Ken was given the responsibility for follow-up action and for making precise recommendations that would prevent a recurrence. This first attempt at being on his own proved successful. His superior responded by further delegation of a similar nature. In time he also increased the complexity of the assignments delegated. The result: after 18 months Ken was promoted to assistant departmental manager. More important, the company had added a valuable asset to its managerial team—a man who, were it not for delegation, might well have left for a different job.

Develop Abilities

This story was contributed by Norbert Vanden Heuvel, vice president, American Family Insurance Group. An executive had a unique opportunity to watch a company grow from an idea in 1961 to a $30 million corporation today. In observing the company's growth he also had a chance to watch the people grow with it. Much of the growth of both must to some extent be attributed to the vice president who was put in charge of the affiliate company. He saw early in the game that he had to develop some key subordinates in a short period of time. His emphasis was on development, and delegation was one of his most important tools.

He feels that good communications with his staff is of extreme importance. He keeps his managers totally informed on all aspects of the business. In that way he can delegate projects that would be beyond the scope of most managers because they would not have the necessary knowledge to carry them out. With follow-ups and status reports he is able to give them the necessary support when they need it. His coaching serves to keep the channels of communication open so that his managers feel completely secure in asking his advice.

One of the men he inherited from another division

seemed to lack organizational ability. In discussing how he should handle this manager, it was suggested that perhaps he had never really been delegated duties properly. His previous superior had given him assignments and then abandoned him. This would have to be changed.

The vice president's approach was to fill in his new manager on the total picture. He then clearly laid out what the manager's responsibilities were. On each project the manager was given he was filled in on the necessary background and told to work it out. He was encouraged to come back with one or more possible solutions and was given all kinds of opportunity for discussion. But it was always clear that it was *his* project. The vice president used coaching and judicious compliments, and built up the manager's confidence with the assurance that his boss would always back him up and discuss problems with him when necessary. As communications improved and rapport developed, this manager began to take hold and was able to see what had to be done and to work out his own program. His development as a manager was most rewarding.

This vice president's ability to delegate so effectively to his subordinates is based on true respect and faith in their abilities. He established strong rapport with his people. He gave them definite responsibilities and permitted them to help set their own accountabilities for results. When this climate is backed by the overriding principle that a manager's job is to develop his subordinates, delegation becomes a truly effective tool.

Develop Through Successive Delegations

George Trombold, director of industrial relations for The Boeing Company, contributed another case history. In early 1965, a large Midwest employer hired a black counselor as a member of its personnel staff. Experience gained during the World War II years had indicated such a person could be a vital cog in the communications process between management and employees, particularly minority employees.

About three years later, as a result of increased involvement of companies with the various federal civil rights agencies, the counselor was promoted to the position of Special Assistant-Equal Opportunity, reporting to the personnel director. With the creation of this position, definite accountabilities were established. The manager was advised that he was not to consider himself a champion for minority groups. Rather, through his normal day-to-day relationships with management and employees, he was, to the best of his ability and with appropriate support, to assure that equal opportunity continued to be a way of life for company employees.

After proving himself in this position, he was appointed vice chairman of the company Equal Opportunity Committee, membership of which consisted of persons designated by the top executives. Through a computerized employee records system, he was provided with frequent reports, including records of all employee transfers, promotions, demotions, and terminations. He was advised to analyze these employee transactions critically to determine, among other things, that minority involvement was not disproportionate in any area. He conducted many discussions with all organizations in this connection.

As his contacts with all levels of company management broadened, he was assigned to assist with the company employment function in addition to his other duties. During the two years this arrangement existed, he became acquainted with management at all levels and the vast majority of the employees, gaining the confidence of all. His personal growth with the company led to a recent promotion to a management position in the Finance Department. His new responsibilities include price estimating within the proposal management organization.

Also, the community, including the minority community, has become aware of this employee's capabilities. Numerous requests have been received for his services on various community affairs committees and boards, the latest being a request from the National Alliance of Businessmen's Youth Motivational Program for him to serve as a national consultant.

This employee's growth over the past five years has been both gratifying and commendable. Throughout this period, his growth was accompanied by the delegation of increasingly complex accountabilities in assignments that can be difficult at best. He is considered a well-rounded, versatile, and valuable employee by everyone who has worked with him in the division.

Don't Develop from Conservatism

A more dramatic illustration of developing through delegation is provided by Charles H. Ford's article, "If You're Problem-Oriented, You're in Trouble" (*Business Management*, February 1969). A manufacturer of metal hardware had been operating with seeming success. His very conservatively run company always made money. His growth was slow and even. The growth rate was consistent with his ambitions for the company.

A new president replaced him upon his retirement. An analysis showed that, although it made money, the company's percentage of profit to sales was steadily declining. Its growth rate was badly outpaced by the growth rate of the industry. If the profit margin continued to shrink, trouble was coming. The new president called a meeting of all executives. "Let your imagination run wild and give me a report in one week of all the changes you'd like to see this company make in ten years so as to become an industry leader," he told them.

Taking the best of these reports, the president convened another meeting. "Instead of making these changes in ten years, we will put them into effect within one year or less," he announced. Accountabilities were delegated, generally to the people whose recommendations he had accepted. "I'm here to help you," he told them. "I'll review your progress on a regular basis but the responsibility is totally yours."

The shock treatment worked. Only one out of nine executives had to be replaced. As an objective-oriented company, its growth is now outpacing the industry's.

When to Practice Participative Management

The question often is asked whether or not effective management means that subordinates should always be permitted to share in decisions affecting them. In other words, is participative management an approach that must be practiced 100 percent of the time to be effective? Can subordinates be developed effectively if they do not participate in every decision having a bearing on their operation? Obviously, time constraints and exigencies of the moment may preclude the opportunity for participation or render it inadvisable. When these questions were posed to J. Clayton Lafferty, president of Human Synergistics, Inc., and a well-respected behavioral scientist, he replied:

When a three-engine Boeing 727 flying at 40,000 feet loses all three engines at once (under normal circumstances the plane could glide for over 130 miles) the captain has ample time for quickly consulting with his co-pilot and flight engineer to get their ideas about the cause and remedy, and to discuss emergency procedures with the stewardesses.

However, if a similar power loss occurred at 500 feet during a takeoff climb, the captain would be ill advised to practice such participative techniques.

Dr. Lafferty's example is dramatic, but it does establish the distinction between desirable management practices to follow under normal circumstances and those that must be waived for the moment based on a higher priority and good business sense.

For example, it would be foolhardy for a president to

delay answering one of the company's top customers for several days just because the sales manager was in Europe and couldn't be reached for discussion prior to making an important decision. Or for a plant manager to delay shutting down a production line that obviously was turning out rejects until he could page and locate the production manager. However, in all but the most extreme cases, the subordinate's growth will be enhanced by giving him the maximum opportunity to help determine the course of action to be taken.

Managers who live and work in the real world have long appreciated the considerable differences in competence and motivation that exist among their subordinate managers. This appreciation permits them to deal realistically with the varying degrees of participation they can permit their subordinates to exercise when determining their accountability. Generally, the three major degrees are illustrated by the following superior to subordinate comments:

Level 1. Here are your objectives! Comment: The boss has the full initiative and no participation is invited or expected.

Level 2. Here are several objectives I believe are realistic for you. What do you think of them? Comment: The boss continues to have the initiative but participation is being invited and encouraged.

Level 3. Let me have your recommended objectives. Comment: Now the initiative has passed to the subordinate and full participation is being encouraged.

Obviously, in-depth delegation contemplates that the vast preponderance of managers will participate at level 3, with a much smaller number operating at level 2 and probably a few at level 1. Level 1 managers may be an exception, but every organization undoubtedly has a few of them. Regardless of how well they may carry out the duties assigned to them by their superior, they constitute a contradiction to delegation and enlightened management.

One of the crucial tests of whether or not delegation has

taken place is the degree to which planning has been decentralized to where each manager does the planning for his own unit. Those who cannot or will not shoulder the initiative for this planning are doubtful managers, at best. Their superiors must try to aid in their development. Failing in this, they must decide whether they, the superiors, can tolerate a situation in which they must continue to do the bulk of the creative thinking and planning for their subordinates.

Developing subordinates through delegation means emphasis on:

1. Joint establishment of definitive accountability for the subordinate
2. Establishment and furtherance by the superior of an atmosphere in which the subordinate is required and permitted to test his abilities under fire
3. Continuous planning, measurement, and adjustment of the subordinate's role based on his demonstrated performance

All three should be the common objectives of the superior and subordinate dedicated to developing men through delegation.

The paramount goal of all development through delegation should be to arrive at an environment in which the manager is able to experience what James Cribbin has referred to as the "eight selfs":

Self-commitment. Since the manager or supervisor has participated in setting the standards, he is likely to accept them and strive to measure up to them.

Self-planning. Knowing the specific results for which he will be held accountable, he can now plan how best to attain them.

Self-motivation. If the standards are realistic, he is challenged to achieve them.

Self-supervision. Since the goals are clear, the burden of supervision is shifted from his superior to himself.

Self-discipline. Like a conscientious athlete, he will tend to discipline himself rather than wait until his boss checks up on him.

Self-management. Standards, in a sense, are a vote of confidence on the part of the superior. The supervisor thus has the freedom to manage his own resources so as to attain his goals.

Self-development. Since standards represent acceptable rather than mediocre performance, he is challenged to stretch to achieve them.

Self-reward. Fulfilling his part of the achievement contract enables him to enjoy the satisfaction that comes from increased competence.[2]

[2] James J. Cribbin, *Effective Managerial Leadership* (AMA, 1972), p. 180.

[15]

EVALUATION
OF DELEGATION

THE PRIMARY thrust and test of delegation may be to determine whether or not the desired result was reached, but evaluation of the effectiveness of the delegation goes beyond the subordinate's end performance. To hold otherwise would be to oversimplify. Complete evaluation involves an examination of the role played by the superior, the role played by the subordinate, and the result itself.

Evaluation should answer the following questions:

1. How well was accountability delegated (primarily the boss's role)?
2. How well was the accountability accepted and carried out (primarily the subordinate's role)?
3. Did the delegation produce the desired results (their joint role)?

The more skillfully and completely the delegation is made, the easier it will be to evaluate. Many of the difficulties encountered in measuring the effectiveness of the dele-

194

gation can be traced to inadequacies in some part of the delegation process. Most often, these inadequacies center around the lack of a clear understanding between the boss and the manager as to the nature and extent of the results that were to be achieved and/or a lack of clear-cut authority to produce the results.

When Evaluation Difficulties Occur

Whenever difficulty is encountered in establishing accountability for a manager or in measuring his performance, special attention should be paid to whether or not one or more of the following questions may apply:

1. Is there a need for the objective, job, or project in question?
2. Is the manager avoiding accountability?
3. Is the authority sufficient for accomplishing the objective?
4. Has an adequate distinction been made between the superior's role and the subordinate's? Whose job is it?

Need for the Job

A medium-size company in Texas had a director of marketing at the headquarters level who had been on the job for about seven years. He probably would still be in the job had it not been for a change in management approach that required all managers to have fixed accountabilities in the form of measurable objectives. The marketing director labored off and on for almost three months trying to spell out his accountability. Finally, he threw up his hands in disgust and informed his boss that the job was of a nature for which accountability could not be fixed.

An analysis of the organization revealed that accountability could not be fixed for that job because it was unnecessary—at least as it was structured. Each of the five divisions had its own marketing and sales organization that reported directly to the division manager, who headed a profit center. Sales were secured on a highly individualized, man-to-man, basis in which company advertising and other forms of pre-selling played a fairly insignificant role. Thus the marketing director could exert little impact on sales and marketing strategy, and his role was limited almost entirely to high-level industry contacts and general activities of a public relations nature. The job was eliminated and all industry contacts and public relations activities were made the accountability of the divisional marketing staffs.

The result was just the opposite in a large grocery sales and distribution company. Its field organization was built around a regional manager concept in which each regional manager had a number of store managers reporting to him. Each local store manager was responsible for running his store and operated on a profit-center basis. The president of this organization questioned how the regional manager could be held accountable for anything except, possibly, the sum of profits for all stores in his region. The analysis in this case revealed a definite need for the regional manager's job and for expanding its accountability. He retained final accountability for total store profits, but became primarily accountable for determining the need for new store openings and planning for them, regional marketing strategy, training of store managers, and other duties that materially increased his accountability.

Evading Accountability

Sometimes it is difficult to evaluate managers because they do not want, or believe it is not possible, to establish the accountability on which they will be measured. Those usually falling into this category are the "business as usual" managers who would be included at the lower end of the scale with respect to achievement orientation. The more achievement-oriented manager insists on strict accountability so that his progress can be measured.

A research executive in a company related to the oil industry had been directing a multimillion-dollar research operation. The company's senior officers began to doubt the value of the return being realized on the research dollar. A general mix of long- and short-term projects coupled with various basic and applied projects made evaluation difficult.

The research vice president was directed to spell out his accountabilities in a way that would make it possible to measure them. His initial reaction was to object strenuously on the basis that his people were creative and couldn't and shouldn't be measured. In effect, he placed himself in the position of saying that the company should continue to provide him with several million dollars each year but shouldn't be concerned with what return it realized on these funds. He was asking the company for a blank check.

This research executive never was able to make the transition from "business as usual" with vague accountability to accountability that could be measured. Unfortunately, his thinking had permeated the entire research function and major surgery on the organization became necessary. He was replaced by a competent manager from outside the company. The new manager, through proper direction of his creative talent and technical expertise, established definite accountabilities for the research department and its managers. Presently, expenditures for research are less, research efforts more nearly match the company's needs, and the results of the research personnel can be evaluated better.

Sufficient Authority

Unfortunately, many superiors make it difficult for themselves when it comes time to evaluate the performance of subordinates. This group violates one of the basic premises of both accountability and evaluation, that the subordinate must have sufficient authority to accomplish his ac-

197

countability. Much to be pitied is the superior who lets his subordinate take refuge in the safe harbor of not having the authority to achieve the result. The subordinate has a built-in, ironclad excuse.

Consider, for example, the sales manager in a well-known construction materials company. This manager has tough, demanding sales targets to achieve, sales objectives that require him to realize a stated percentage of building materials used for all new housing starts in his area. His boss is a highly methodical individual who believes in making certain that every detail has been checked and is perfect before action is taken. He requires all proposals for sales above a certain amount to be submitted to him for final approval prior to the sales manager being able to bid for the business.

Housing builders and contractors don't have an abundance of patience when it comes to dealing with suppliers; they don't have to because of the highly competitive nature of the building supply business. What they can't get from one supplier they can quickly get from another. They demand prompt service, quick decisions, and on-time deliveries. Their substantial investment in labor and equipment and construction financing costs make them extremely intolerant of delays when dealing with sales personnel from suppliers.

This particular sales manager insists that he has lost countless large-volume sales because he has to write up sales above a certain volume and submit them to higher authority before he can make a firm bid. He says sales managers from competing companies are running rings around him because they enjoy more authority to make prompt, binding decisions on the spot. To the extent his reasons are valid, the ability to evaluate his performance is seriously weakened.

This manager's reasons for not performing have placed the responsibility squarely on the shoulders of his superior. The superior can transfer the responsibility back to the manager by granting him the authority necessary to accomplish his objectives. Then the subordinate will be placed in the position of having authority he must exercise. His safe harbor will have gone by the boards.

Whose Job Is It?

Fuzzy evaluation often results when the superior and subordinate each is responsible for a portion of the same or interrelated project or objectives. For example, a superintendent and his foremen are frequently both accountable for machine utilization and costs.

The wrapping department of a candy manufacturing company serves as an example of confused accountability and evaluation. There is an extremely high degree of correlation among (1) high-speed equipment, (2) number of breakdowns, and (3) potential costs of these disruptions to production. Getting a wrapping line back on stream at the earliest possible time becomes a critical accountability for all managers concerned.

The potential costs of breakdowns must be weighed against the relatively high costs of maintaining a corps of highly qualified and expensive technical personnel in reserve to resolve the breakdowns. In the case under discussion, the superintendent had three of these machine technicians reporting directly to him rather than having one reporting to each of the five foremen who were in charge of the five different wrapping lines. When a breakdown occurred, the foreman contacted the superintendent and requested a technician.

The number of breakdowns increased as the company continued to speed up the machines to maintain its competitive cost position, and it became increasingly difficult to fix the accountability for the costs of breakdowns. Were the costs being incurred by delays on the part of the superintendent in assigning the technicians or by his failure to hire and train personnel with the required abilities to diagnose

199

the trouble and correct it in the shortest possible time? Did the costs occur because the foremen did not maintain the machines properly or practiced sloppy operating procedures? Or were the superintendent and the foremen both at fault? At best, these questions are difficult to answer because of the confused, mingled accountability.

The Superior's Role

The superior should take a hard look at how well he has delegated or allowed delegation to take place when he evaluates the delegatee and the results achieved. He should ask whether he has made a clear-cut delegation and promoted a management atmosphere in which the delegation could be nurtured and grow. In essence he should review each of his actions and determine if they are consistent with his role as described in Chapter 7. If he has not fulfilled his own role, he must make allowances for any defects in accomplishment by his subordinate. If, for example, he has failed to grant enough authority to his managers he must make allowances for any weaknesses in their performance that might have been caused by this lack of authority.

Earl Brooks suggests the following criteria for determining how well the boss has delegated:

1. Do you and your subordinates agree on what results are expected of them?
2. Do you and your subordinates agree on measure of performance?
3. Does each of your subordinates feel that he has sufficient authority over his personnel?
4. Does he feel that he has sufficient authority concerning finances, facilities, and other resources?
5. Within the past six months what additional authority have you delegated?
6. What more does each of your subordinates think should be delegated to him?

7. Is accountability fixed for each of your delegated responsibilities? Is your follow-up adequate?
8. Are you accessible when your subordinates need to see you?
9. Do your subordinates fail to seek or accept additional responsibility?
10. Do you bypass your subordinates by making decisions which are part of their job?
11. What interferes with the effective use of your management time?
12. Do you do things your subordinates should do? Why?
13. How could you best improve your delegation?
14. If you were incapacitated for six months who would take your place?
15. Ask each of your subordinates individually, "What could I do, refrain from doing, or do differently which would help you do a better job?" [1]

Evaluating the Results

The most effective evaluation measures actual results as compared with the specific accountability (expressed as measurable objectives) of the manager. Until the widespread adoption of the management by objectives system, evaluation tended to be based on personality traits. It is unfortunate, but the personality-trait-oriented evaluation method continues to be used by many organizations, seriously weakening their delegation process. No matter how skillfully the other components of delegation have been handled, it is not possible to measure the results of the delegation process when this type of evaluation is used.

Let's assume that a subordinate was given clear-cut responsibility, and that he and his boss agreed on the specific accountability he would have. The accountability required the subordinate, among other things, to reduce his depart-

[1] Earl Brooks, "Get More Done—Easier," *Nation's Business* (October 1962), pp. 1–5.

mental costs by 12 percent, and he was given the necessary authority. However, when the target period was over, his boss relied on the personality-oriented evaluation. He measured him on highly subjective factors like initiative, grasp of function, ability to get along with people, degree of cost consciousness, loyalty, health, and potential for advancement. Chances are that the manager's real accomplishments, or lack of them, will be completely lost in the maze of these highly subjective, irrelevant evaluation factors.

The most effective approach to evaluation measures the subordinate's accomplishments on an objectives versus results basis. The entire evaluation process is oriented to measuring results; personality factors enter into the process only when they may be exerting a material impact on the ability of the manager to achieve his objectives. For example, a manager may be realizing his anticipated results by practicing poor human relations that might drive his employees to a costly strike later on.

Table 15-1 is a sample of the form used to measure managers on a results-oriented basis. The form records only the end result of the manager's actions. To get a complete picture of the manager's accomplishments, it is usually necessary to analyze the end results further. Aspects to be considered should include:

1. Quantitative aspects. (Was cost reduced 5 percent as planned?)
2. Qualitative aspects. (Have good relations been established with Department X? Has an evaluation technique been established?)
3. Deadline considerations. (Was the deadline beaten? Was it met?)
4. Proper allocation of time to given objectives.
5. Type and difficulty of objectives.
6. Creativity in overcoming obstacles.
7. Additional objectives suggested or undertaken.

8. Efficient use of resources.
9. Use of good management practices in accomplishing objectives (cost reduction, delegation, good planning, and so on).
10. Coordinative and cooperative behavior; avoidance of conflict-inducing or unethical practices, and so on.

Tosi et al. summarize by saying

Evaluation and measurement, therefore, require considering both means and ends, being concerned with both the objective (number, type, difficulty, etc.) and the means to its achievement (cost, cooperativeness, time consumed, etc.). Unless this is done, an important opportunity to communicate expectations, feed back performance results, and set effective goals may be lost. It must be

Table 15-1. Results-oriented review and evaluation form.

| OBJECTIVES | MEASURE | RESULTS ACHIEVED | | | |
		1ST QTR.	2ND QTR.	3RD QTR.	TOTAL* YEAR
1. Reduce scrap costs by 10% over 1971	1. Total cost of materials and labor for units that cannot be reworked and total labor costs for all units that can be reworked	T†	O	T	Scrap costs reduced by 11%
2. Increase yield of apple orchard by 6%	2. Bushels per acre of salable fruit	O	T	T	Yield increased by 5%

* Record of performance for the total year is to be used as the basis for compensation reviews and other personnel actions.
† Codes facilitating management by exception:
T = on target, no action necessary
O = off target, action necessary

203

fully understood that evaluation has obvious links to action plans, as well as to desired end states.[2]

Counseling for Results

Once the results of the manager's achievements have been evaluated, the final chore of the superior is to translate them into meaningful and constructive suggestions for the continuing development of the subordinate.

Constructive counseling should be based on a philosophy of helping the subordinate to improve and not on tearing him down or berating him for his failures. Emphasis should be on improving future performance rather than criticizing past failures. One of the aids to putting counseling on a constructive, rather than destructive, basis is to evaluate and counsel subordinates more than once a year. Annual sessions almost invariably culminate in the manager accepting the session as a criticism of his previous performance. This, coupled with evaluations based on personality traits, leaves the subordinate in a defensive position; he is never really sure how the boss will evaluate his personality. A better way to counsel is to:

Evaluate and counsel the subordinate at least four times a year; more if it is considered beneficial.

Use results-oriented evaluation.

Concentrate the session on the planning and reviewing of objectives.

In this combination of future orientation and more frequent reviews the superior focuses on helping the manager lay out his objectives and plans for the remainder of the year. Poor planning can be spotted before it becomes a reality and causes problems to develop. Also, the four quarterly

[2] H. L. Tosi, J. R. Rizzo, and S. J. Carroll, "Setting Goals in Management by Objectives," *California Management Review* (Summer 1970), p. 76.

reviews help break the task up into more easily analyzed and managed units. Changing priorities and/or changing needs of the organization can be isolated and allowances made for their impact. They are less likely to be overlooked than with a once-a-year review.

When properly done, the evaluation phase of delegation should provide both the subordinate and the superior with a gauge of how well each has performed his respective role. Also, it should provide them with a measure of how well they worked together to achieve the desired results. Each will be made aware of his strengths and weaknesses in delegation and of how these impacted on the role of the other party to the delegation contract. Both will have guides for improving their delegation skills in the future.

The evaluation phase should make it abundantly clear to both parties, if any doubt existed, that delegation doesn't flow only from higher to lower levels. It flows both ways and involves a continuous interaction, with each level making the necessary inputs for improving the process.

The appendix provides a checklist for managers to use as a guide in evaluating how well they delegate. After the manager has completed the checklist, he should have at least one of his subordinate managers complete the same checklist and evaluate the superior's delegation practices through his eyes. Comparing the answers of the two can provide the superior with considerable food for thought and future action.

[16]

THE DEMAND FOR ACCOUNTABILITY AND PARTICIPATION

THE DEMAND for accountability on the part of managers has never been greater. Both the marketplace and owners are increasingly demanding more of business managers. Managers of churches and other religious institutions are being required more often to justify to their congregations the effectiveness with which stewardship is being met. Citizens, taxpayers, and organized pressure groups are demanding that government agencies and departments achieve meaningful, worthwhile goals. Students and parents alike are exerting comparable pressures on school managers and administrators. Volunteer groups are being required to document the reason for their existence. Fund-raising organizations are no longer being supported blindly just because their cause is honorable. Social agencies in general are discovering that appreciable demands are being made upon them for accountability. Even the military finds itself in the position of having its objectives and performance questioned from many quarters.

206

At the same time, traditional power and authority relationships are crumbling. The readiness to salute and the prompt "yes sir" are fast disappearing from the military. Dogma and blind faith in one's superiors are no longer widely accepted by many levels of church management. Both students and teachers are rebelling against the traditional, all-knowing approach of school administrators. The actions and attitudes of employees and managers, especially middle-level managers, indicate an appreciable amount of unrest and dissatisfaction with jobs in which they do not have a major voice. Finally, even the traditional power-authority relationship between parent and child has been replaced by a new order of things.

These broad and sweeping departures from the past, that is, the demand for stricter accountability by owners and interested parties and the demand for a larger voice in self-determination by those who work for the organization, suggest a common theme as one means of meeting the dual demands. Delegation designed to achieve definite desired results for the organization and optimize these results by providing a vehicle for utilizing the talents of all managers can do much to satisfy the demand for stricter accountability. Delegation that affords all managers a significant voice in self-determination can go far in helping to make their efforts more satisfying and rewarding.

The Challenge

Currently, much is being written and spoken regarding the impact of an age of technology on the motivation of employees, particularly those on machine-paced or highly systematized operations. Motivation is alleged to have suffered as the result of employees losing their identity to machines, of not being able to demonstrate their individuality, and of having systems control them rather than having them control the system. The increasing impact of this lack of interest in the job is being translated into undesirable costs resulting from higher absentee and tardiness rates, greater turnover, lower product quality, lower productivity, and, in some cases, outright sabotage.[1] Considerable time and money are being devoted to finding means for enlarging or enriching the employee's job so that he will again take pride and interest in his job and in the organization for which he works. Any solutions coming from these efforts must face the almost overwhelming obstacle of having to be financially feasible in light of economic constraints imposed by domestic and foreign competition and the consumer's willingness and ability to foot the increased bill that undoubtedly would be part of the package.

Unfortunately, the deluge of attention to the plight of the poor, disinterested employee has overshadowed the fact that many managers—particularly those at the lower and middle management levels—are experiencing a similar plight. Mobility of managers is a good indication. A large percentage no longer find it attractive to stay with one organization for long periods of time. Turnover among managers has increased, particularly during times of prosperity. Mobile pensions that permit carrying pension credits from one employer to the next have become more attractive. The increasing appeal to managers and professionals of unions and quasi-union organizations is another indication.

Managerial absenteeism is on the upswing. An increasingly large number of managers are leaving corporate life completely and switching to teaching, social work, or running their own small businesses. A large steel company reported recently that the problem has become so acute that it had to conduct a full-scale productivity improvement program for its management personnel. The rat race of corporate life has become less attractive to the younger generation upon whom business depended for its managers of the

---

[1] For a dramatic example of the problem, see "Luddites in Lordstown," by Barbara Garson, *Harper's* (June 1972), pp. 68–73.

future. Finally, the managerial demands of ten to fifteen years ago for higher pay and pay-related benefits have lessened in importance in favor of more opportunity for managerial freedom and individuality.

The failure of management to take positive action to alleviate the proportions of this problem as it impacts on its managers will find it in the unenviable position of being able to retain only those managers who are prone to answer "yes" and being unable to attract competent managers for the future.

The Opportunity

Fortunately for management, the alternatives for meeting the challenge of enriching managerial jobs are greater than those currently being considered in conjunction with employees. The constraints on managerial action are less.

The possibilities brought forth to date for enriching employee jobs have posed added cost burdens. Schemes such as decreasing the amount of specialization; that is, allowing the employee to follow through with a product and work on several succeeding stages of it rather than concentrating almost exclusively on one operation, substitute higher costs for lower ones. In many instances, such as automobile production, the anticipated cost increase would seriously affect consumer demand. Whether these initial cost increases would be offset by subsequent cost decreases from increased employee motivation, lower turnover and absentee rates, and similar advantages is debatable.

No such debate is needed for affecting considerable job enrichment for managers. No cost increases are necessary. What is necessary is a positive dedication by management at all levels to provide all managers with the opportunity, encouragement, and methods by which they can demonstrate their own individuality in a way that is supportive of the organization's needs. Much of this can be accomplished by permitting the manager to tailor his job to his capability and, to a more limited degree, his ambitions. The latter constitutes delegation in action.

Delegation in Action

Effective delegation carries with it the promise that the individual manager will be given the widest possible latitude to determine his own job and that all the managers in the organization, acting together like this, will achieve results considerably in excess of those realized by managers not operating in a comparable manner. Tailoring the job to the man requires a complete departure from the historical approach, in which the totality of the job was described and then a manager was selected for the job. Tailoring the job reverses the emphasis. Minimal data and job requirements are specified—hopefully only enough to outline the parameters of the job. The manager has the opportunity to add the real meat to the skeleton by having a major voice in determining his responsibility; accountability; authority; operating plans, methods, and management style; and feedback.

Responsibility

Of the five components listed for tailoring the job, responsibility is the least flexible in terms of the manager's opportunity to influence it. Much of the content is assigned by the superior when he places the man in the job. In other words, the incumbent is told, "You are the director of purchasing. You are in charge of the purchasing function." Thus, the scope of the major portions of his job has been set. Boundaries have been established within which he must operate.

However, even here the manager has at least some opportunity to influence content. For example, he may determine that the operation would be more productive if he were given the additional responsibility for warehousing and inventory control. If so, it would be incumbent upon him to recommend and justify this additional assignment. Many managers can and should enlarge their jobs in this manner.

Accountability

This aspect of tailoring provides the manager with the greatest possible opportunity to make his own job. Even though two managers may have identical responsibility, the accountability of each can vary by infinite degrees, depending upon the abilities and ambitions of each.

Take the job of purchasing director discussed in the preceding paragraphs. One man filling this job regards it in a rather loose, business-as-usual fashion. He regards his accountability as consisting primarily of routinely processing purchase requisitions and orders, placing orders with vendors, and making certain materials are delivered on schedule. His actions place him in the administrator-buyer category.

Another purchasing director on the same job is a real manager and believes he is employed to contribute to profits by the way he handles the purchasing job. He regards processing paperwork, placing orders, and insuring deliveries as only the routine part of his job, some of the tools he uses in his trade. He considers his true accountability as composed of generating profits in areas like utilizing value engineering to get an equally satisfactory, substitute product at a lower cost; getting an identical product from a supplier with valuable services or better warranties than those provided by another supplier; receiving the cost advantage of volume discounts but getting the vendor to do most of the warehousing by delivering in small quantities as needed; and establishing the lowest practical inventory levels to keep working capital requirements at a minimum.

In the first instance, the job has made the man. In the second, the man has made the job and the benefits to the organization are infinitely greater.

Authority

Here again authority should flow with the man by being tailored to his accountability. The more timid, ineffective manager isn't overly fond of being delegated much authority. He'd rather run to the boss for advice and have someone to check with and share the blame if things don't go well. To him, minimal authority—the more minimal the better—provides a shelter for his weaknesses. It gives the superior a measure of comfort too, because he knows the weak manager can't undertake anything major without prior checking.

A competent, achievement-oriented manager would be driven crazy by the same minimal authority. He would feel hamstrung by his inability to carry out the accountabilities he is capable of delivering. If he didn't resign, he would quickly reach the conclusion that his organization was nonprofit, even if it intended otherwise.

Planning and Action

The next step in tailoring the job to the manager by delegation involves giving him the latitude to do his own planning, to execute his own actions, and to practice his own management style. This phase of tailoring takes cognizance of the reality that all managers will approach matters in a different way. All managers might quarrel with the approach and style their associates use, but there should be no quarrel with the end objective of reaching optimum results. The brusque, head-on approach of some managers would fail miserably if practiced by others, and the brusque manager might be completely ineffective if he tried to emulate those whose style is subtler. Barring the use of unethical or unsound management practices, the manager should be free to pursue flexible solutions to his objectives and problems.

Feedback

The feedback discussed in detail in Chapter 12 is the final step in the tailoring process. A definite void exists when an organization goes through the other steps in tailoring but fails to provide ample data for planning, decision making, and measurement of actual achievement compared with plans.

The most effective feedback results from the conscious effort to collect all data with the individual manager in mind—true responsibility accounting. Data collected primarily for the manager's superior or for product-costing purposes will not meet the manager's need. He, his boss, and the financial personnel all must contribute to make it meaningful for the manager who needs it. Then the same data can be adapted for other uses.

Total Enrichment

Any consideration of job enrichment must be keyed to bottom-line accounting. An enrichment that benefits the manager must also benefit the organization. Otherwise, enrichment becomes an end in itself and subject to the same fate that usually befalls any endeavor in which the mean becomes confused with the end.

Delegation serves both the manager and his organization when the delegator and the delegatee, working together, succeed in putting into consistent practice actions in which:

1. The major objectives of the organization are broken down into manageable, challenging tasks for all levels of management.

213

2. All managers are encouraged to contribute to the maximum of their abilities and ambitions.
3. Managers are given the freedom to act consistent with their abilities.
4. Managers know what is required of them and are able to stand on their own two feet.
5. Managers have a major voice in determining what is required of them.
6. A system of recognition and rewards plays its necessary role in motivating acceptance of accountability and promoting better performance.
7. The combined efforts of all managers culminate in a synergistic result in which the total is greater than the sum of the individual inputs.
8. Managers haven't yet been where they're going.

The total benefits that accrue from these actions are the real end purpose and reward of no-nonsense delegation.

APPENDIX

How Much Do I Delegate?

Checklist and Action Plan

1. Have I taken all vacations in the last five years? _____
   Action Plan _____

   _____

2. Do I work longer hours than those reporting to me? _____
   Action Plan _____

   _____

3. Do I usually do work at home? _____
   Action Plan _____

   _____

4. Do I get more than two phone calls a week at home? _____
   Action Plan _____

   _____

5. Do I frequently come into the office when it's closed? _____
   Action Plan _____

   _____

6. Am I usually behind in my work? _____
   Action Plan _____

   _____

7. Do I measure my success primarily by time worked or
   accomplishment? _____
   Action Plan _____

   _____

8. Do my people request advice once or twice a day? _____
   Action Plan _____

   _____

9. Do I have limited time for outside interests? _____
   Action Plan _____
   _____

10. Are job descriptions for my people of the activity type? _____
    Action Plan _____
    _____

11. Do my people recommend at least 75 percent of their
    objectives? _____
    Action Plan _____
    _____

12. Does the organization chart for my unit accurately
    reflect responsibility? _____
    Action Plan _____
    _____

13. Do my people consistently make recommendations to
    me? _____
    Action Plan _____
    _____

14. Do they know specifically the results they must achieve? _____
    Action Plan _____
    _____

15. Are they consistently qualified for promotions when
    promotions occur? _____
    Action Plan _____
    _____

16. What have I reserved strictly to myself? _____
    Action Plan _____
    _____

17. Has authority been clearly defined? _____
    Action Plan _____
    _____

18. Is the authority in writing? _____
    Action Plan _____
    _____

19. Did my people recommend it to me? _____
    Action Plan _____
    _____

20. How much authority codes A and B do they have?[1] _____
  Action Plan _____

21. How much authority code C do they have?[1] _____
  Action Plan _____

22. Do they consistently exercise their authority without checking with me? _____
  Action Plan _____

23. Has authority been tailored to accountability? _____
  Action Plan _____

24. Do I consult with them prior to setting my own objectives? _____
  Action Plan _____

25. Do their questions to me involve details or policies? _____
  Action Plan _____

26. How many times have I overruled them in the past year? _____
  Action Plan _____

27. How often do I check on their work? _____
  Action Plan _____

28. Is all of my checking done overtly? _____
  Action Plan _____

29. How many staff meetings do I hold a month? _____
  Action Plan _____

[1] Authority codes:
  A, manager may act and need not report.
  B, manager may act but must report to his superior as soon as possible.
  C, prior approval by superior is required.

30. When I ask a question about matters two levels down from me:
    a. From whom do I expect answers? _____
    b. Who usually answers? _____
    Action Plan _____

    _____

31. Do I evaluate based on personality traits or results? _____
    Action Plan _____

    _____

32. Do I reward based on results? _____
    Action Plan _____

    _____

33. Do I reward in proportion to results? _____
    Action Plan _____

    _____

34. Do my subordinates have effective responsibility accounting? _____
    Action Plan _____

    _____

35. Do they have a major voice in determining their feedback? _____
    Action Plan _____

    _____

36. Are decisions made at the lowest level at which all information is available? _____
    Action Plan _____

    _____

37. Is my department plagued by slow decision making? _____
    Action Plan _____

    _____

38. Do my people do their own planning or is it done centrally? _____
    Action Plan _____

    _____

39. Are important decisions postponed when I'm away? _____
    Action Plan _____

    _____

40. Do I check in with the office when I'm away? _____
    Action Plan _____

41. May my secretary schedule appointments for me? _____
    Action Plan _____

42. Do I review all of my correspondence before it is mailed? _____
    Action Plan _____

43. Is the development of people a major consideration when I delegate? _____
    (a) Do I really know the strengths and weaknesses of my people? _____
    (b) On what do I base this judgment? _____
    (c) Have I delegated enough to them to justify this judgment? _____
    Action Plan _____

44. Do my people consistently achieve the desired results? _____
    Action Plan _____

45. Do I permit my people to select their own means to agreed-upon ends? _____
    Action Plan _____

46. Do I grant my people the right to be wrong? _____
    Action Plan _____

47. How often do I make changes affecting them without giving them the right to be heard? _____
    Action Plan _____

48. If I were a subordinate would I be happy working for myself? _____
    Action Plan _____

49. What percentage of my job do I really delegate? _____
    Action Plan _____
    _____

50. Would my subordinates agree with the accuracy of this
    percentage? _____
    Action Plan _____
    _____

51. Could I increase my productivity and lessen my mana-
    gerial difficulties if I delegated more? _____
    Action Plan _____
    _____

Suggestion: Prior to beginning your action plan, would you be willing to permit your subordinates to answer the same questions but
from the standpoint of how they see you?

INDEX

abilities, development of, 186–187

accountability
  vs. authority, 140
  control and, 19
  delegation and, 13, 135–136, 194
  demand for, 206–214
  evasion of, 196–197
  final, 13–15, 135–136
  in job description, 111–115
  key-results areas in, 116
  for marketing director, 118
  opportunity and, 211–212
  prime, 14
  problems of, 199–200
  vs. responsibility, 111–115
  statement of, 115–116

achievement
  misinterpretation of, 77
  recognition of, 77

agreement, need for in delegation "contract," 47–48

American Family Insurance Group, 186

assets, utilization of, 22–23

authority
  vs. accountability, 140
  action and, 140
  in billion-dollar corporation, 142–143
  budgeting, 145–146
  categories of, 143–152
  commensurate, 138–139
  in decision making, 170–171
  delegation and, 13

authority (*continued*)
    expression of, 143–152
    general, 144
    granting or securing of,
        141–142
    inadequate, 197–199
    lack of, 63
    management action and, 153
    mistakes in, 138–141
    opportunity and, 212
    personal nature of, 141
    procedural, 145
    questionnaire on, 153–154
    ratification of, 140
    results from, 137–154
    revising of, 152–154
    sample lists of, 146–151
    specific granting of, 92, 145

blame, vs. credit, 95–96
Boeing Company, 187–188
Borenstine, Alvin, 179 n.
boss, delegatee's relationship
    and reporting to, 102, 105–
    106
Brooks, Earl, 200–201
bulging briefcase, power delega-
    tion and, 35–36
business enterprise, society and,
    4
Business Management, 189

Carroll, S. J., 204 n.
communication, clarity in, 91
compensation, motivation
    through, 20–21
completed staff action, concept
    of, 107–108
consultation, prior use of, 87
control, span of, *see* span of con-
    trol

controlling, vs. delegation, 18–
    19
controls
    inadequate, 57
    management by exception in,
        158–161
    measure in, 162
    objectives in, 161–165
    product emphasis in, 155–157
    responsibility accounting in,
        157–158
    routine goals in, 166
    specific, 57–58
    tailoring of, 58–59, 161–164
    wrong emphasis in, 155–157
cooperative goal setting, 76
costs, as social phenomenon, 5
credit, vs. blame, 95–96
Cribbin, James J., 192–193

Davis, Ralph C., 127
decision analysis, 175–176
decision making
    authority and, 170–171
    committees in, 173–174
    confused responsibility in,
        169–170
    delegation and, 13
    faulty, 169
    inadequate data in, 171–172
    management atmosphere in,
        172
    misplaced, 38–39
    positive, 177–179
    slowness in, 37–38
    technical staff and, 174–175
    time limits in, 172–173
decision-making power, testing
    of, 176–177

decision-making process, rekindling of, 178
delegatee
feedback to, 104–105
first job of, 106
initiative of, 100–102
personal goals of, 103–104
relations with boss, 102–103
role of, 100–108
self-development in, 106–107
delegation
advance action in, 83–84
agreement in, 47
"boss" in, 102–103
checklist of action plan in, 215–220
consistency in, 97
credit vs. blame in, 95–96
criteria in, 200–201
decision making and, 168–179
defined, 11
development of managers through, 180–193
disorganized effort in, 13–14
distance in, 26–27
dual nature of, 101
ease of managing and, 30–31
effective, 8
elements of, 12–13
evaluation of, 194–205
in foreign operations, 24–25
foundation for, 64–79
four-level, 72–74
freedom in, 88
gaps and laps in, 85–86
of good and bad, 81–82
gradualness in, 83
ineffectiveness in, 5–7
job description in, 109–123

job enrichment and, 213–214
key-results areas in, 116, 119, 128–130
larger organizations and, 29–30
as legal contract, 47, 100
by levels, 124–136
management atmosphere and, 69–79
management hierarchy and, 124–136
at management level, 86
management styles and, 65–69
need for, 182–190
opportunities and challenge in, 210–213
paper shuffling as, 32–33
as philosophy or way of life, 64
planning and, 17–18
plant manager in, 132–134
poor, 32–45
power transfer in, 87–88
prerequisites for, 79
president and, 50
prior consultation in, 87
product diversity and, 28–29
professional manager and, 25–26
realistic nature of, 103
reasons for, 16–31
redefining of, 11
results in, 101, 201–204
review and evaluation form for, 203
right man in, 80–81
role of, 1–15
secrecy and, 42–43
selectivity in, 89

delegation (*continued*)
  for specific results, 84–85
  subordinates' ball carrying
    and, 39–40
  successive, 187–189
  suggested items for, 99
  superintendent and, 134–135
  trust in, 94
  truths of, 80–89
  uniqueness and, 128
  in vacuum, 61–62
  whole action in, 84
delegator
  role of, 90–99
  support from, 96
development
  of abilities, 186–187
  vs. babying, 183
  from confusion, 185–186
  from conservatism, 189–190
  through delegation, 180–193
  eight "selfs" in, 192–193
  through problem solving, 184
  through successive delega-
    tions, 187–189
directing, vs. delegation, 13
disorganized effort, 43–44
distance, delegation and, 26–27
Drucker, Peter F., 3–4
Dubinsky, David, 41
dynamic controls, establishment
  of, 155–167
  see also controls

evaluation
  of delegation, 194–205
  difficulties in, 195–200
events, "normal distribution" of,
  4

failure, fear of, 76–77
feedback
  delegatee and, 104–105
  management atmosphere and,
    71
  in tailoring process, 213
final accountability
  concept of, 13
  vs. prime accountability, 135
financial vice president, ac-
    countability statement for,
    117
Ford, Charles H., 189
foreign operations, delegation
  in, 24–25
future, for achievement-ori-
    ented management, 78

gaps, avoidance of, 85–86
Garson, Barbara, 208 n.
General Electric Company, 181
goal setting, cooperative, 76

Human Synergistics, Inc., 75,
  190

International Ladies Garment
  Workers' Union, 41

job confusion, poor delegation
  and, 60
job description
  activities vs. results in, 54
  changing priorities in, 54–55
  delegation and, 109–123
  improvement in, 56
  inadequate controls in, 57–59
  individual and, 56–57
  key components of, 112
  key-results areas in, 119–121

nondescriptive, 51–57
performance standards and
121–123
responsibility vs. accountability in, 111–115
typical, 52–53
weaknesses in, 110–111
job enrichment, delegation and, 213–214

key-results areas
accountability and, 116
delegation based on, 128–130
first- and second-line supervisors in, 134–135
selection of, 119
in statement of accountability, 116
in store operations, 130–132

labor, as fixed cost, 5
Lafferty, J. Clayton, 75–79, 190
Laird, D. A., 82, 89, 126–127
Laird, E. C., 82, 89, 126–127

Machiavelli, Niccolò, 178
MacKenzie, R. Alec, 127
McMurry, Robert N., 61 n.
management
balanced, 10
challenge and opportunity in, 207–210
defined, 1–2
delegation by, 8–9
"ease" of, 30–31
effort vs. paybacks in, 6–7
nonpermissive, 15
size of enterprise and, 6–7
management atmosphere, 69–79

decision making and, 172
feedback in, 71
recognition and rewards in, 74–75
management by exception, control through, 158–161
management capabilities, 27–28
management development, 182–193
see also development
management hierarchy, delegation in relation to, 124–136
management level
delegation and, 86
typical, 73
management style
changes in, 69
delegation and, 65–69
supportive foundation for, 66
manager(s)
change and, 68–69
compensation for, 20–21
as "controller," 67
defined, 1–15
delegation and, 1–15
as delegator(s), 90–99
development of through delegation, 180–193
evaluation of, 19–20
as motivator, 67–68
operations planning by, 71
problems of, 3–4
professional, 25–26
responsibility vs. accountability in, 111–115
see also superior; supervisor
managerial absenteeism, increase in, 208
managing
vs. operating, 127

managing (*continued*)
vs. permissiveness, 15
vs. running, 2–3
marketing director, statement of accountability for, 118
misdirection, at top level, 9
mistakes, magnitude of, 70
misunderstanding, poor delegation and, 46–48
money expenditures, poor delegation and, 40–41
monitoring, delegation and, 13
motivation, 23–24
loss of, 207–208

no-nonsense delegation, defined, 15
"normal distribution," fallacy of, 4–5

objectives, poor delegation and, 37
Odiorne, G. L., 167 n.
operation, vs. management, 127
organization, achievement-oriented vs. nonachievement oriented, 76–79
organization chart, delegation and, 48–51
organization level, delegation in relation to, 124–136
organization size, delegation and, 29–30
overcontrol, poor delegation and, 34–35

participation, demand for, 206–214
participative management, effectiveness of, 190–193

performance standards, job description and, 121–123
permissiveness, vs. managing, 15
personnel manager, improper asset utilization by, 10
planning
delegation and, 13, 17–18
opportunity in, 212–213
poor or weak, 33–34
plant manager
delegation in reference to, 132–134
responsibility of, 72
policy defects, poor delegation and, 37
poor delegation
"bulging briefcase" and, 35–36
causes of, 46–63
constant pressure in, 36
detailed job knowledge and, 42
frequency of orders in, 34
isolation and, 60–61
job confusion and, 60
job content and, 61–62
lack of authority and, 63
lack of objectives and, 37
lack of policy in, 37
lack of understanding in, 46–48
misplaced decision making and, 38
misunderstandings in, 45–48
nondescriptive job description in, 51–57
overcontrol in, 34–35
paper shuffling in, 32–33
president as one-man company in, 50

product costing and, 59
quoting boss in, 41
"slippery organization chart"
    and, 48–51
slow decisions in, 37–38
span of control in, 39
spending money and, 40–41
symptoms of, 32–45
undercontrol in, 35
poor planning, 33–34
president, organization chart
    and, 50
prime accountability
    concept of, 14
    vs. final, 135–136
priorities
    control objectives and, 162
    establishment of, 12
    in job description, 54–55
problem solving, development
    through, 184
product costing, poor delega-
    tion and, 59
product diversity, delegation
    and, 28–29
professional manager, delega-
    tion and, 25–26
profit planning, delegation and,
    17–18

responsibility
    decision making and, 169–
    170
    delegation and, 13
    opportunity in, 210–211
    problems of, 199–200
responsibility accounting, con-
    trol in, 157–158
results
    authority and, 137–154
    vs. methods, 93

Rizzo, J. R., 204 n.
"running," vs. managing, 2–3

secrecy, delegation and, 42
self-commitment, 192
self-defeating attitudes, 23–24
self-development, 193
self-direction, of subordinate,
    23–24
self-discipline, 192
self-improvement, belief in, 76
self-management, 193
self-motivation, 192
self-planning, 192
self-reward, 193
self-supervision, 192
Smyth, R. C., 147
social phenomenon, costs as, 5
society, business enterprise and,
    4
span of control, poor delegation
    and, 39
staff action, 107–108
standards, control and, 19
statement of accountability,
    115–116
store operations, organization
    of, 130–132
subordinance, level of compe-
    tence in, 81
subordinate(s)
    ball carrying by, 39–40
    criticism of, 36–37
    development of, 21–22
    freedom of action in, 88
    items for delegation to, 99
    knowledge of by superior,
    97–98
    participation by, 92–93
    recommendations by, 94–95
    responsibility sharing with, 89

subordinate(s) *(continued)*
  review of, 93
  selection of, 80–81
  self-direction in, 23–24
  support of, 96
  transfer of power to, 87–88
  see also delegatee
success, hope vs. probability of,
  77–78
superior
  communication by, 91
  consistency in, 97
  development of people by,
    98–99
  evaluation of delegation by,
    200
  knowledge of subordinates
    by, 97–98
  review of results by, 93
  role of, 90–99

support from, 96–97
trust by, 94

task completion, importance of,
  76
Tosi, H. L., 204 n.
Trombold, George, 187–188

undercontrol, poor delegation
  and, 34–35
uniqueness, delegation based
  on, 128

Vanden Heuvel, Norbert, 186
vice president, accountability
  for, 117

wasted effort, hierarchy of, 8–
  10
whole action, delegation of, 84
Wright, Moorehead, 181 n.